DELICIOUSLY HEALTHY COOKING FOR DIABETE

BY YAEL AVITAL

President and Chief Executive Officer: Rick Barton
Vice President of Editorial: Susan White Sullivan
Vice President of Sales: Mike Behar
Vice President of Operations: Jim Dittrich
Vice President of Finance: Laticia Mull Dittrich
Vice President of Purchasing: Fred F. Pruss
National Sales Director: Martha Adams
Creative Services: Chaska Lucas
Information Technology Director: Hermine Linz
Controller: Francis Caple
Retail Customer Service Manager: Stan Raynor
Director of Designer Relations: Cheryl Johnson
Special Projects Director: Susan Frantz Wiles
Art Publications Director: Rhonda Shelby
Director of eCommerce-Prepress Services: Mark Hawkins

Produced for Leisure Arts, Inc. by Penn Publishing, Ltd.
www.penn.co.il
Editor-in-Chief: Rachel Penn
Editor: Deanna Linder
Design and layout: Michal & Dekel
Photography: Danya Weiner
Styling: Orya Geva

This publication contains the opinions and ideas of the author. It is intended to provide helpful and informative material on the subjects addressed in the publication. It is sold with the understanding that the author and publishers are not engaged in rendering medical, health, or any other kind of personal professional services in the book. The reader should consult his or her medical, health, or other competent professional before adopting any of the suggestions in this book or drawing inferences from it. The author and publishers specifically disclaim all responsibility for any liability, loss or risk, personal or otherwise, which is incurred as a consequence, directly or indirectly, of the use and application of any of the contents of this book.

PRINTED IN CHINA
ISBN-13: 978-160900-406-4
Library of Congress Control Number: 2011934382

Cover photography by Danya Weiner

DELICIOUSLY HEALTHY COOKING FOR DIABETES

BY
YAEL AVITAL

TABLE OF CONTENTS

SALADS

MAIN COURSES

ACKNOWLEDGMENTS

I would like to especially thank the following people, without whose help, I could not have written this book:

Rachel and Elan Penn, who asked me to author this book. I came to realize that writing this book sums up years of my knowledge, work and love for cooking.

Danya Weiner and Orya Geva for the beautiful photos and styling.

Deanna Linder for editing.

Ruth Moshe, clinical dietitian, for her support and guidance and especially for helping me write the introduction.

My many friends and relatives, who gave me ideas for recipes and tasted them when necessary.

My family—the real judges of my cooking:

To my husband Arik, who not only lent his support along the way, but was the most meticulous proofreader.

To my daughter Dganit without whose help, with ideas and cooking, this book could have never come to be.

To my son Oren, who encouraged me and helped along the way, solving software problems.

ABOUT THE AUTHOR

Yael Avital, M.Sc. received her master's degree in Food Engineering from the Institute of Technology in Haifa, Israel and is a senior food engineer with over 23 years' experience in the field of baking technology. Yael specializes in the development of baked goods for special dietary needs, such as gluten-free, sugar-free and reduced calorie foods. She has developed hundreds of products for leading international food companies. In 1991 Yael co-authored the book, *Sugar-Free Cooking and Diet*, a 300-recipe cookbook for diabetes.

MY CONNECTION WITH DIABETES

When I was twelve years old, my best friend was diagnosed with type 1 diabetes, which at the time was very difficult to treat. I so admired her mother, who took the time to prepare meals to fit her daughter's needs, and who excelled in the cake department (especially apples, I remember). Several years later, one of my sisters married a marvelous man, who also suffered from type 1 diabetes. As an avid baker and cook, remembering the mother of my childhood friend, I tried to make him desserts, cakes and cookies to fit his dietary needs.

Fast forward several years later when, as a mother of three, I started my master's degree in Food Engineering. During a course in nutrition and diabetes, the professor encouraged me and another student, a dietitian, to join forces with two of the leading doctors in diabetes care and write a cookbook for people with diabetes. In 1991, the book *Sugar-free Cooking and Diet* was published. Once I finished graduate school and began working in the food industry, I was drawn to the field of baked goods and began to develop recipes for reduced-calorie, sugar-free cakes and cookies specifically for people with diabetes.

Over the years I developed a whole range of products for a company which manufactures special products for diabetes, most of which received the stamp of approval from the American Diabetes Association. I also created sugar-free and reduced-calorie dessert recipes for several newspapers and magazines. One of my sons, a computer engineer, developed software which calculates the nutritional data of recipes. The software uses the U.S. Department of Agriculture (USDA) Standard Reference database and is adapted to the requirements of the U.S. Food and Drug Administration (FDA).

While writing this book, my husband was diagnosed with type 2 diabetes. The need for the recipes I was writing became a reality for our home. These recipes were tested first on the software to make sure that their nutritional value and calorie requirements were suitable for people with diabetes. Once they passed the test, my daughter (who has exceptionally creative cooking skills) and I cooked our way through each recipe, while family and friends helped by tasting them. My husband, who helped proofread, was taught a valuable lesson in diabetes nutrition.

I hope that you, the reader, enjoy the tremendous effort put into creating these healthy, tasty and easy recipes, all suited to the dietary requirements of diabetes.

Yael Avital

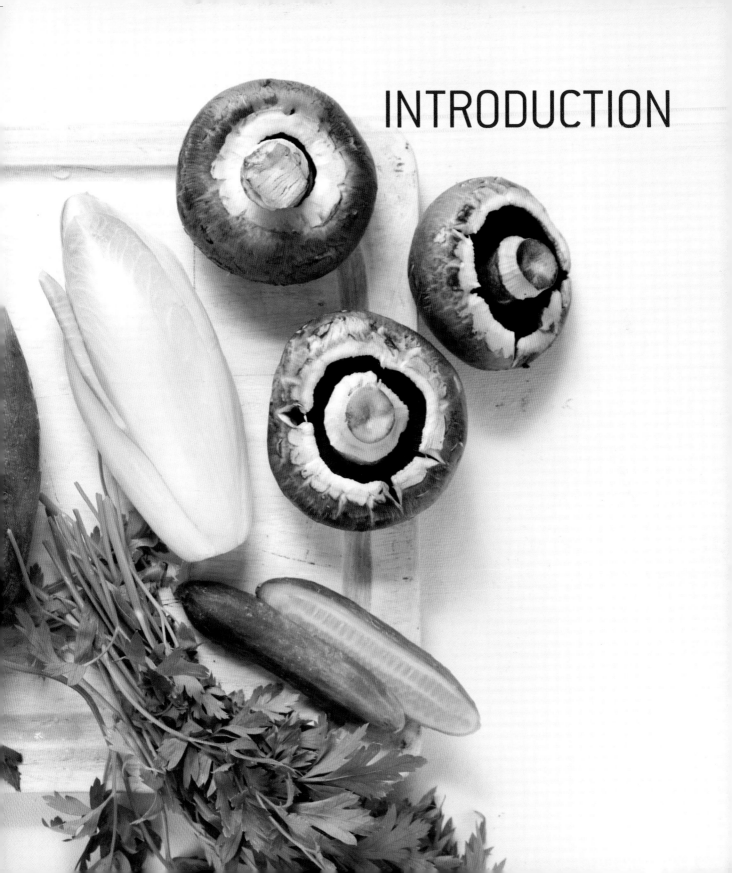

INTRODUCTION

EAT YOUR VEGETABLES

Eating lots of vegetables is one of the central recommendations conveyed in most diabetes diet guidelines. My love for fruits and vegetables, along with the dietary recommendations, drove me to create recipes filled with fresh produce. Cooking with a variety of vegetables enriches the taste of the recipe as well as contributing to the nutritional value, by adding fiber, vitamins and minerals.

All of the recipes in the book are easy enough for everyone to prepare at home. Most of the recipes can be stored in the refrigerator for a few days after cooking; some even get tastier over time. Some of the recipes may also be frozen. Storing instructions are listed after each recipe; if there is no storage instruction, the recipe should be consumed upon preparing.

NUTRITION INFORMATION

The recipes in this book have important nutrition information for developing a healthy-eating plan. Each recipe includes:

— The Nutrition Facts Label, in accordance with FDA requirements, displays nutrient information per serving for each recipe. In addition, it provides the % Daily Value (%DV) each nutrient contributes to your diet. These numbers are based on a 2000-calorie diet. A nutrient is low if 5% or less and high if 20% or more.

— The Carbohydrate Choice number and the Diabetes Exchange List data are provided to help count carbohydrates.

Both the nutrient information and carbohydrate count should be used in conjunction with the Dietary Guidelines for Americans developed by the USDA and the U.S. Department of Health and Human Services (HHS).

CARBOHYDRATE COUNTING

Once people are diagnosed with diabetes, one of the first issues they encounter is trying to work out the proper consumption of carbohydrates. People with type 2 diabetes need to do two important things following their diagnosis: lose weight and count carbohydrates.

WHAT ARE CARBOHYDRATES?

Once digested, carbohydrates are broken down into glucose which causes the blood sugar to rise. However, it is still important to eat carbohydrate containing foods as they provide energy and important nutrients our bodies need. The key is how much carbohydrate to eat, and that amount depends on your individual calorie needs and nutrition goals (i.e. if you are a vegetarian, if you have high cholesterol levels, etc.). Talk with your healthcare provider about how much carbohydrate you might need on a daily basis.

Carbohydrate counting is a useful tool which helps people with diabetes manage blood sugar levels, when used in conjunction with medication and exercise.

One carbohydrate "choice" is equal to 15 grams of carbohydrate. Foods which contain up to 10 grams of carbohydrate are considered half a carbohydrate choice. Foods which contain less than 5 grams are considered zero or "free". For example, 15 grams of carbohydrate is the equivalent of: 1 slice of bread, $1/3$ cup cooked rice, $1/3$ cup cooked pasta, 1 small apple, 1 small orange or $1\frac{1}{4}$ cups of strawberries. Refer to the Exchange Lists on page 176 for more examples.

Most of the recipe servings in this book do not exceed one carbohydrate choice.

SUGGESTED MEAL PLANS

These are suggested meal plans, compiled from recipes in this book. The nutritional data refers to one serving.

EASY FISH MEAL

Page No.	Recipe	Serving Size	Calories	Fat (grams)	Carbohydrates (grams)	Carbohydrate Choice	Dietary Fiber
107	BAKED TILAPIA	7 oz.	190	7	3	0	1
78	WALNUT & VINAIGRETTE SALAD	1 cup	80	6	5	½	2
132	BROCCOLI WITH ALMONDS	1 cup	110	8	7	½	3
141	AROMATIC RICE PILAF	1 cup	110	2	24	2	3
157	FRUIT SALAD WITH HOMEMADE BERRY SAUCE	1½ cups	60	0	15	1	2
	Total		**550**	**23**	**54**	**4**	**11**

FANCY FISH MEAL

Page No.	Recipe	Serving Size	Calories	Fat (grams)	Carbohydrates (grams)	Carbohydrate Choice	Dietary Fiber
35	PEAR VICHYSSOISE SOUP	¾ cup	80	2	16	1	3
92	BAKED SALMON IN PARCHMENT PAPER	4 oz.	160	6	5	0	1
73	BEET, CARROT & APPLE SALAD	1 cup	90	4	13	1	2
70	PICKLED CUCUMBER & DILL SALAD	½ cup	10	0	3	0	1
151	BROWN RICE WITH SWISS CHARD & SPINACH	1 cup	110	1	20	1½	3
160	COFFEE BAVARIAN CREAM WITH CARAMELIZED WALNUTS	1 cup	100	4	8	½	1
	Total		**550**	**17**	**65**	**4**	**11**

QUICK CHICKEN MEAL

Page No.	Recipe	Serving Size	Calories	Fat (grams)	Carbohydrates (grams)	Carbohydrate Choice	Dietary Fiber
34	FENNEL & RED PEPPER SOUP	1 cup	40	0	7	½	3
83	CABBAGE & BABY RADISH SALAD	1 cup	50	2	7	½	2
111	LEMON CHICKEN SCALLOPINI	5½ oz.	210	5	4	0	1
145	WHOLE-WHEAT PASTA WITH ZUCCHINI & SAGE	1½ cups	200	4	35	2½	5
159	FRUIT SALAD SOUFFLÉ	1 cup	130	3	22	1½	3
	Total		**630**	**14**	**75**	**5**	**13**

WEEKDAY BEEF MEAL

Page No.	Recipe	Serving Size	Calories	Fat (grams)	Carbohydrates (grams)	Carbohydrate Choice	Dietary Fiber
31	VEGETABLE BROTH	1 cup	50	2	6	½	4
118	ROASTED SIRLOIN WITH TOMATOES	8 oz.	200	7	6	½	1
77	CABBAGE & CARROT SALAD	1½ cups	70	3	10	1	4
135	GINGER CAULIFLOWER	1 cup	63	2	9	0	4
151	BROWN RICE WITH SWISS CHARD & SPINACH	1 cup	110	1	20	1½	3
162	HOMEMADE STRAWBERRY ICE CREAM	½ cup	34	0	7	½	1
	Total		**613**	**15**	**58**	**4**	**17**

PASTA MEAL

Page No.	Recipe	Serving Size	Calories	Fat (grams)	Carbohydrates (grams)	Carbohydrate Choice	Dietary Fiber
36	MINESTRONE SOUP	1½ cups	130	1	25	1½	6
80	GRAPEFRUIT & AVOCADO SALAD	1½ cups	80	4	8	½	2
95	SPICY SHRIMP IN COCONUT MILK	2 cups	170	7	3	0	1
143	WHOLE-WHEAT PENNE IN TOMATO SAUCE	10 oz.	180	3	31	2	4
157	FRUIT SALAD WITH HOMEMADE BERRY SAUCE	1½ cups	60	0	15	1	2
	Total		**620**	**15**	**82**	**5**	**15**

ASIAN BUFFET

Page No.	Recipe	Serving Size	Calories	Fat (grams)	Carbohydrates (grams)	Carbohydrate Choice	Dietary Fiber
26	THAI CHICKEN & LEMON SOUP	1¼ cups	70	4	2	0	1
74	INDONESIAN SHRIMP & BANANA SALAD	1½ cups	120	3	16	1	2
75	COCKTAIL SAUCE	1½ Tbs.	30	2	2	0	1
57	VIETNAMESE EGGROLLS	4 oz.	130	2	23	1½	2
55	STUFFED BELL PEPPERS*	6 oz.	70	2	11	½	2
52	CUCUMBER RAITA	1 cup	60	1	7	½	1
141	AROMATIC RICE PILAF	1 cup	110	2	24	2	3
	Total		**590**	**16**	**85**	**5½**	**12**

* ½ pepper per serving

EASY MEAL FOR ENTERTAINING

Page No.	Recipe	Serving Size	Calories	Fat (grams)	Carbohydrates (grams)	Carbohydrate Choice	Dietary Fiber
28	THAI PUMPKIN SEAFOOD SOUP	1 cup	80	3	6	¹/₂	1
115	TURKEY CURRY	1¹/₂ cups	180	6	11	1	1
152	INDIAN RICE	2 cups	180	2	37	2¹/₂	4
170	CHESTNUT & WALNUT COOKIES	2 cookies	110	8	9	¹/₂	4
	Total		**550**	**19**	**63**	**4¹/₂**	**10**

WEEKEND BRUNCH

Page No.	Recipe	Serving Size	Calories	Fat (grams)	Carbohydrates (grams)	Carbohydrate Choice	Dietary Fiber
44	OLIVE & PUMPKIN SEED SPELT ROLLS	1 roll	70	2	13	1	3
47	MUSHROOM SCONES	1 scone	60	1	11	1	2
51	TUNA SALAD WRAPS	1 wrap	30	1	0	0	1
54	AVOCADO DIP	2 Tbs.	60	4	2	0	2
87	TANGY CHICKEN SALAD	1¹/₂ cups	160	6	14	1	2
172	APPLE MOUSSE	¹/₂ cup	40	0	10	1	1
	Total		**420**	**14**	**50**	**4**	**11**

VEGETARIAN FEAST — RICH IN DIETARY FIBER

Page No.	Recipe	Serving Size	Calories	Fat (grams)	Carbohydrates (grams)	Carbohydrate Choice	Dietary Fiber
32	MUSHROOM SOUP	³/₄ cup	60	2	7	¹/₂	4
148	QUINOA ANTIPASTI	10 oz.	250	12	28	2	6
84	FRESH BEET SALAD	1 cup	70	3	12	1	3
167	BAKED APPLES WITH CRANBERRY SAUCE	4 oz.	60	2	13	1	3
	Total		**440**	**19**	**60**	**4¹/₂**	**16**

DIETARY FIBER

Dietary fiber includes all parts of plant foods that your body can't digest or absorb. Fiber has several important roles in maintaining health.

INSOLUBLE FIBER VS. SOLUBLE FIBER

There are two types of fiber: insoluble (does not dissolve in water) and soluble (does dissolve in water). Insoluble fiber promotes the movement of food through your digestive system and increases stool bulk, so it is beneficial to the health of your colon. Whole grains, wheat bran, brown rice, nuts, seeds and many vegetables are good sources of insoluble fiber. Because soluble fiber dissolves in water and forms a gel-like substance, it can help lower blood cholesterol and blood sugar levels. Foods such as beans, oats, barley, apples, citrus fruits and carrots provide soluble fiber.

WHY DIETARY FIBER IS IMPORTANT

— Helps lower blood cholesterol and control blood sugar levels. Soluble fiber may help lower cholesterol levels by lowering low-density lipoprotein (LDL) cholesterol. Soluble fiber also slows the absorption of sugar.

— Helps prevent constipation by increasing bulk and softening the stool. Fiber may also help lower your risk of developing hemorrhoids and diverticulosis.

— Helps reduce blood pressure and inflammation, which is also good for heart health.

— Helps with weight loss by increasing feelings of satiety and decreasing calorie intake since high fiber diets tend to be lower in calories for the same volume of food.

Current recommendations for intake of dietary fiber is 38 grams per day for men aged 50 and younger, 30 grams per day for men aged 51 and older, 25 grams per day for women aged 50 and younger, and 21 grams per day for women aged 51 and older.

WHOLE GRAINS

Whole grains are an important source of dietary fiber, rich in important plant-based nutrients (phytonutrients), vitamins and minerals. Replacing processed grains (refined grains) with whole grains in your diet may help control blood glucose, lower cholesterol and aid weight loss. Blood sugar rises slower after a meal containing whole grains than after eating processed grains (refined grains).

It is currently recommended for most people to eat a minimum of 3 ounces of whole grains (such as 1/2 cup cooked brown rice, 1/2 cup cooked whole-wheat pasta and 1 slice whole-wheat bread) each day.

SUGARS & SWEETENERS

Some of the recipes in the book make use of a small amount of honey or brown sugar. This amount is barely noticeable in a single portion. If you still want to replace sugars, use two teaspoons of sugar substitute instead of one tablespoon of honey.

Sucralose, sold under the brand name Splenda® can be used in baking. Be sure not to use aspartame-based sweeteners when cooking, as they break down during the cooking process, resulting in a loss of sweetness.

I prefer to use sucralose-based, stevia-based and erythritol-based sweeteners. (Erytrithol is not a real sweetener. It is a sugar substitute, nearly calorie free, and has to be combined with a sweetener – like in Truvia®).

ALLERGENS

The recipes in this book do not contain warnings about allergens. If you are allergic to a certain food, please be aware of the ingredients prior to preparation.

SALT, SODIUM & POTASSIUM

In recent years, following evidence of an acute rise in blood pressure in the population, as well as the discovery of a direct link between salt intake and blood pressure, a demand has arisen to reduce the sodium content in food. Sodium is required for a large number of critical body functions. When we sweat, salt is emitted from the body. The role of healthy kidneys is to discharge the excess salt from the body. High blood pressure is a contributor to cardiovascular disease, strokes and kidney failure. For this reason, the Academy of Nutrition and Dietetics (formerly the American Dietetic Association) recommends the reduction of salt consumption. The Dietary Guidelines for Americans also recommend reducing daily sodium intake to 2300 mg or less, depending on an individual's risk factors. It is important to remember that much of the sodium in our diet is already in the food itself, either naturally or through processing.

In this book, I have made great efforts to reduce the amount of salt in the recipes. However, no one wants to eat food that is not tasty! Therefore I have also gone to great lengths to find different ways of creating tasty flavors without using large amounts of salt.

We can get used to less salt in food, and it is essential to do so when your blood pressure is high and the doctor recommends such a diet. The many vegetables in these recipes also aid in this mission of sodium reduction. The use of vegetables and lemon allow for better tasting food, but with less salt. There are vegetables that naturally contain a small amount of sodium. The amount of sodium has been calculated in each nutrition facts table.

In addition, it has been found that eating potassium-rich fruits and vegetables aid in blood pressure reduction. Recipes in this book include these and other potassium sources: beets, garbanzo beans, bananas, lentils, tomatoes, cucumbers, broccoli and oranges.

It is preferable to use fresh or frozen vegetables. Canned goods, unless otherwise stated, contain high levels of salt. It is highly recommended that you note the amount of sodium indicated on the ingredients of different foods. For example, make sure you use the kind of tomato paste that contains almost no sodium.

Written with assistance by clinical dietitian Ruth Moshe, RD, CDE.

SOUPS

FRENCH ONION SOUP

This is a reduced calorie version of the classic calorie rich soup and is great to serve on a cold wintery evening.

INGREDIENTS

For the stock:

6 cups water

1 carrot, peeled and coarsely chopped

2 celery ribs, coarsely chopped

1 teaspoon salt

3 bay leaves

3 whole allspice berries

For the soup.

2 tablespoons butter

1 tablespoon olive oil

4 yellow onions, thinly sliced

1 teaspoon salt

Freshly ground pepper

$1/4$ teaspoon ground nutmeg

1 tablespoon whole-wheat flour

$1/2$ cup dry red wine

For garnish:

1 tablespoon Parmesan cheese, grated

8 SERVINGS

SERVING SIZE: 1 cup, 240 g, 8 oz.

		% Daily Value
Calories per serving	110	
Calories from fat	40	
Total Fat	5 g	7%
Saturated Fat	2 g	10%
Cholesterol	10 mg	3%
Sodium	120 mg	5%
Total Carbohydrates	11 g	4%
Sugars	4 g	
Dietary Fiber	2 g	8%
Protein	4 g	
Vitamin A		35%
Vitamin C		16%
Calcium		12%
Iron		2%
Carbohydrate Choice	1	

EXCHANGES: 2 Vegetable, 1 Fat

PREPARATION

1. Place all ingredients for the stock in a large saucepan and bring to a boil over high heat. Reduce heat, cover and simmer for about 1 hour. Strain stock, reserving liquid, and discarding vegetables.

2. Heat the butter and olive oil in a Dutch oven over medium heat and add the onions. Sauté for about 7-10 minutes, until the onions are translucent. Add the salt, pepper and nutmeg and continue to cook for another minute. Add the flour and stir until well blended.

3. Add the prepared stock to the onions and cook for 20 minutes. Remove from heat, add the wine and stir until combined.

4. Top with grated Parmesan cheese and serve.

✳ Soup may be stored in an airtight container in the refrigerator for up to 5 days.

CHICKEN BROTH

Chicken soup is "medicine" for colds, the flu, cold winter days, or when you are simply not feeling well. One serving of this soup and you will start to feel better — guaranteed!

This is also a great base for other soups in this chapter. Substitute the chicken with one chicken bone and two turkey necks for lower fat content.

INGREDIENTS

1¼ pounds skinless chicken legs
1 parsnip, peeled and sliced
3 celery ribs, sliced
1 cup parsley, coarsely chopped
2 carrots, peeled and sliced
1 yellow onion, peeled and quartered
5 cups water
3 bay leaves
3 whole allspice berries
1 teaspoon salt
1 cup fresh dill (optional)

20 SERVINGS

SERVING SIZE: 1 cup, 210 g, 7 oz.		
Calories per serving	80	% Daily
Calories from fat	20	Value
Total Fat	2 g	3%
Saturated Fat	0 g	0%
Cholesterol	30 mg	10%
Sodium	355 mg	15%
Total Carbohydrates	6 g	2%
Sugars	2 g	
Dietary Fiber	2 g	6%
Protein	11 g	
Vitamin A		66%
Vitamin C		10%
Calcium		4%
Iron		7%
Carbohydrate Choice	½	
EXCHANGES: 1 Vegetable, 1 Lean Meat		

PREPARATION

1. Place all ingredients in a large stockpot and cook for about 1 hour, until chicken is cooked through and vegetables are tender.

2. Serve broth along with vegetables or strain broth and store.

* Broth may be stored in an airtight container in the freezer for up to 2 months.

THAI CHICKEN & LEMON SOUP

This is a classic Thai soup, but the diet version. Fresh lemongrass and kaffir lime leaves may be found in gourmet or Asian markets. Coconut milk or coconut cream, found in many Thai dishes, contain a large amount of saturated fat. This soup contains light coconut milk which has a much lower fat content than regular coconut milk. This soup gets better with time.

INGREDIENTS

6 cups strained
   Chicken Broth (see page 25)
3 cups light coconut milk
4 pieces lemongrass, about 3 inches long, lightly bruised
1 inch fresh ginger, peeled and cut into strips
8 kaffir lime leaves
2 cups white mushrooms, sliced
$1/2$ cup baby corn, sliced into halves

10 oz. boneless, skinless chicken breasts, cut into strips
$1/3$ cup fresh lemon juice

For garnish:
1 tablespoon red pepper flakes (optional)
1 bunch green onions, diagonally sliced, green parts only
$1/2$ cup cilantro leaves

10 SERVINGS

SERVING SIZE : 1^1/4 cups, 240 g, 8 oz.

		% Daily Value
Calories per serving	70	
Calories from fat	40	
Total Fat	4 g	6%
Saturated Fat	4 g	20%
Cholesterol	10 mg	3%
Sodium	360 mg	15%
Total Carbohydrates	2 g	1%
Sugars	0 g	
Dietary Fiber	1 g	4%
Protein	5 g	
Vitamin A		5%
Vitamin C		34%
Calcium		2%
Iron		1%
Carbohydrate Choice	0	

EXCHANGES: $1/2$ **Vegetable,** $1/2$ **Fat,** $1/2$ **Lean Meat**

PREPARATION

1. Place the chicken broth, coconut milk, lemongrass, ginger and kaffir leaves in a large stockpot and bring to a boil. Lower heat to medium and cook for 10 minutes.

2. Strain the soup broth into a clean stockpot and add the mushrooms, baby corn and chicken. Cook for an additional 7-10 minutes, until the chicken is cooked through. Add the lemon juice, stir and remove from heat.

3. Serve into individual bowls and garnish with the red pepper flakes, green onion slices and cilantro leaves.

✳ Soup may be stored in an airtight container in the refrigerator for up to 5 days.

¤ *Thai Chicken & Lemon Soup*

THAI PUMPKIN SEAFOOD SOUP

Pumpkin is a great natural source of antioxidants and is low in calories. You can make a vegetarian version of this soup by omitting the seafood and using water or vegetable stock instead of chicken broth.

INGREDIENTS

1 yellow onion, coarsely chopped
1 yellow bell pepper, coarsely chopped
1 green chili pepper, coarsely chopped
2 garlic cloves
2 cups water
1 cup strained Chicken Broth (see page 25)
2 tablespoons fish sauce
1 pound pumpkin, peeled, seeded and cut into 1-inch cubes
2 cups light coconut milk
1 packet sugar substitute
Freshly ground pepper
10 oz. mixed seafood (squid, shrimp, clams, mussels), fresh or frozen and thawed

For garnish:
1 red chili pepper, thinly sliced
10 basil leaves

10 SERVINGS

SERVING SIZE: 1 cup, 200 g, 7 oz.

Calories per serving	80	% Daily
Calories from fat	20	Value
Total Fat	3 g	4%
Saturated Fat	2 g	10%
Cholesterol	20 mg	7%
Sodium	120 mg	5%
Total Carbohydrates	6 g	2%
Sugars	2 g	
Dietary Fiber	1 g	4%
Protein	7 g	
Vitamin A		61%
Vitamin C		35%
Calcium		3%
Iron		5%

Carbohydrate Choice   1/2

EXCHANGES: 1/2 Starch, 1/2 Lean Meat

PREPARATION

1. In a food processor, blend together the yellow onion, bell pepper, green chili pepper, garlic, and 1/2 cup of the water until reaching a paste consistency.

2. In a large stockpot, bring the remaining 1 1/2 cups water, chicken broth, prepared paste and fish sauce to a boil.

3. Lower heat to medium, add the pumpkin and continue cooking for 10-15 minutes, until the pumpkin is tender.

4. Add coconut milk, sugar substitute and black pepper. Taste and season accordingly.

5. Add the seafood and cook for 3-4 minutes, until cooked through. Garnish with red chili pepper and basil and serve.

✳ Soup may be stored in an airtight container in the refrigerator for up to 5 days.

¤ *Thai Pumpkin Seafood Soup*

THAI SHRIMP SOUP

Traditionally this is a very spicy soup. You can control spiciness by gradually adding the chili pepper, until reaching the desired level. This soup is low in calories but packed with flavor. Although shrimp contains high cholesterol levels, it is low in saturated fat.

6 SERVINGS

SERVING SIZE: 1¹/₄ cups, 240 g, 8 oz.

		% Daily Value
Calories per serving	60	
Calories from fat	10	
Total Fat	1 g	1%
Saturated Fat	0 g	0%
Cholesterol	50 mg	17%
Sodium	405 mg	17%
Total Carbohydrates	2 g	1%
Sugars	3 g	
Dietary Fiber	1 g	4%
Protein	9 g	
Vitamin A		35%
Vitamin C		50%
Calcium		5%
Iron		7%

Carbohydrate Choice 0

EXCHANGES: ¹/₂ Vegetable, 1 Lean Meat

INGREDIENTS

2 cups strained Chicken Broth (see page 25)

2 cups water

3 pieces lemongrass, each about 3 inches long, lightly bruised in a mortar with a pestle

10 kaffir lime leaves

4 cups white mushrooms, sliced

1 cup cherry tomatoes, halved

1 tablespoon Thai fish sauce

¹/₃ cup fresh lemon juice

¹/₂ cup cilantro leaves, finely chopped

3 tablespoons green onions, thinly sliced

1 red bell pepper, sliced into thin strips

1 red chili pepper, thinly sliced (optional)

2 teaspoons salt

2¹/₂ cups large uncooked shrimp, peeled with tails left on and deveined

For garnish:

1 tablespoon red pepper flakes (optional)

1 bunch green onions, diagonally sliced, green parts only

¹/₂ cup cilantro leaves

PREPARATION

1. Place the chicken broth, water, lemongrass, and kaffir leaves in a large stockpot and bring to a boil. Lower heat to medium and cook for 10 minutes.

2. Strain the soup into a clean stockpot and add the mushrooms, tomatoes, fish sauce, lemon juice, cilantro leaves, green onion, red bell pepper and red chili pepper, and cook for 8-10 minutes. Season with salt.

3. Add the shrimp and cook for about 5 minutes, until they become opaque. Serve into individual bowls and add the red pepper flakes, chopped green onion and cilantro leaves.

＊ Soup may be stored in an airtight container in the refrigerator for up to 5 days.

VEGETABLE BROTH

You can prepare this recipe as a hearty soup, serving the vegetables along with the broth. You can also strain the soup and render only the broth for a stock, which may be frozen and used in many other dishes which call for vegetable stock.

INGREDIENTS

2 tablespoons olive oil

1 yellow onion, coarsely chopped

2 leeks, sliced into $1/4$-inch slices, white and light green parts only

2 carrots, peeled and sliced into $1/4$-inch slices

1 celeriac, peeled and cut into 1-inch cubes

2 parsnips, peeled and sliced into $1/4$-inch slices

$2^1/2$ cups cabbage, sliced

1 bay leaf

3 whole allspice berries

3-4 sprigs of thyme (optional)

$1/2$ teaspoon turmeric (optional)

8 cups water

3 zucchini, sliced into $1/2$-inch slices

1 cup parsley, coarsely chopped

10 SERVINGS

SERVING SIZE: 1 cup, 210 g, 7 oz.

		% Daily Value
Calories per serving	50	
Calories from fat	20	
Total Fat	2 g	3%
Saturated Fat	0 g	0%
Cholesterol	0 mg	0%
Sodium	60 mg	3%
Total Carbohydrates	6 g	2%
Sugars	4 g	
Dietary Fiber	4 g	16%
Protein	2 g	
Vitamin A		53%
Vitamin C		10%
Calcium		6%
Iron		4%

Carbohydrate Choice $1/2$

EXCHANGES: $1^1/2$ Vegetable

PREPARATION

1. In a large stockpot, heat the olive oil and add the onion and leeks, and then sauté for about 5 minutes until translucent.

2. Add all the remaining ingredients, excluding the zucchini and parsley, making sure that the water just covers the vegetables. Add more water if needed.

3. Bring to a boil, reduce heat and cook for 30 minutes.

4. Add the zucchini and parsley and cook for an additional 10 minutes, until the zucchini is tender.

5. Serve as a soup or strain and render the liquid for stock.

✳ Broth may be stored in an airtight container in the freezer for up to 2 months.

MUSHROOM SOUP

Mushrooms contain very few calories, but add lots of flavor to soups and stews. One serving of this soup contains 4 grams of fiber which is 16% of the daily recommended intake. Use a mix of different types of mushrooms for a richer taste.

INGREDIENTS

1 tablespoon butter
2 tablespoons all-purpose flour
2 garlic cloves, minced
8 cups fresh mushrooms (white, cremini, portobello, oyster), thinly sliced
2 cups strained Vegetable Broth (see page 31)
2 cups water
$1/2$ teaspoon fresh thyme leaves
$1/4$ teaspoon ground nutmeg
Freshly ground pepper

For garnish:
Sprigs of fresh thyme

6 SERVINGS

SERVING SIZE: $3/4$ cup, 150 g, 5 oz.

		% Daily Value
Calories per serving	60	
Calories from fat	20	
Total Fat	2 g	3%
Saturated Fat	1 g	5%
Cholesterol	5 mg	2%
Sodium	20 mg	1%
Total Carbohydrates	7 g	2%
Sugars	3 g	
Dietary Fiber	4 g	16%
Protein	3 g	
Vitamin A		0%
Vitamin C		48%
Calcium		8%
Iron		13%

Carbohydrate Choice $1/2$

EXCHANGES : $1 1/2$ Vegetable, $1/2$ Fat

PREPARATION

1. In a large stockpot, heat the butter on medium heat and add the flour and garlic, while constantly stirring for 1 minute.

2. Add the mushrooms and sauté for about 5 minutes, until softened. Add the vegetable broth, water, thyme leaves, nutmeg and pepper and continue cooking for 10-15 minutes.

3. Garnish with thyme sprigs and serve.

✳ Soup may be stored in an airtight container in the refrigerator for up to 4 days.

¤ *Wild Mushroom Soup*

FENNEL
&
RED
PEPPER
SOUP

The fennel in this soup does wonders — once cooked, it adds to the creamy consistency without the strong anise flavor typically associated with fennel. You can use yellow, orange or green bell peppers instead of red ones.

INGREDIENTS

2 fennel bulbs, trimmed and sliced
2 red bell peppers, sliced
1 yellow onion, sliced
4 cups strained Vegetable Broth (see page 31)
1/4 cup fresh lemon juice
1 1/2 teaspoons salt

For garnish:
1/4 cup dill, chopped

10 SERVINGS

SERVING SIZE: 1 cup, 210 g, 7 oz.

		% Daily Value
Calories per serving	40	
Calories from fat	0	
Total Fat	0 g	0%
Saturated Fat	0 g	0%
Cholesterol	0 mg	0%
Sodium	255 mg	11%
Total Carbohydrates	7 g	2%
Sugars	3 g	
Dietary Fiber	3 g	12%
Protein	2 g	
Vitamin A		35%
Vitamin C		10%
Calcium		5%
Iron		6%

Carbohydrate Choice 1/2

EXCHANGES: 1 1/2 Vegetable

PREPARATION

1. Place the fennel, bell peppers, onions and vegetable broth in a large stockpot and cook on high heat until boiling. Reduce heat to medium and cook for 30-40 minutes until the vegetables are tender.

2. Add the lemon juice and salt. Using an immersion blender, blend the soup until smooth.

3. Garnish with dill and serve.

✷ Soup may be stored in an airtight container in the refrigerator for up to 4 days.

PEAR VICHYSSOISE SOUP

Vichyssoise is a French-style soup typically made with leeks, onions, potatoes, heavy cream and chicken stock, served either hot or cold. In this version, the leeks and onions star on their own, without the heavy cream, of course, but with the addition of pear, which makes this version slightly sweet and creamy.

INGREDIENTS

2 tablespoons butter
3 shallots, finely chopped
3 cups leeks, thinly sliced, white parts only
2 ripe pears, peeled, cored and chopped
3 cups water
1 teaspoon salt
Pinch of ground nutmeg

For garnish:
1 ripe pear, peeled, cored and thinly sliced

8 SERVINGS

SERVING SIZE: 3/4 cup, 180 g, 6 oz.

		% Daily Value
Calories per serving	80	
Calories from fat	20	
Total Fat	2 g	3%
Saturated Fat	1 g	4%
Cholesterol	5 g	2%
Sodium	245 mg	10%
Total Carbohydrates	16 g	5%
Sugars	4 g	
Dietary Fiber	3 g	12%
Protein	2 g	
Vitamin A		20%
Vitamin C		10%
Calcium		6%
Iron		4%
Carbohydrate Choice	1	

EXCHANGES: 1 Vegetable, 1/2 Fat, 1/2 Fruit

PREPARATION

1. In a large stockpot, melt the butter over medium heat, add the shallots and leeks and sauté for about 5 minutes, until translucent.

2. Add the pears, water, salt and nutmeg and cook for 30 minutes. Use an immersion blender to blend the soup until smooth.

3. Garnish with pear slices and serve warm or cold.

✱ Soup may be stored in an airtight container in the refrigerator for up to 4 days.

MINESTRONE SOUP

This soup is filled with a variety of vegetables. The soup also contains beans, a great source of fiber, making it a meal in itself.

INGREDIENTS

1 tablespoon olive oil

2 yellow onions, coarsely chopped

1 celeriac, peeled and cut into 1-inch cubes

3 celery ribs, coarsely chopped

2 zucchini, coarsely chopped

4 carrots, peeled and cut into 1-inch cubes

3 red bell peppers, cut into 1-inch cubes

$1/2$ cup small dried white beans (such as cannelloni), soaked in water overnight and drained

1 cup crushed tomatoes

5 cups water

1 teaspoon salt

Freshly ground pepper

1 bunch parsley, chopped (optional)

10 SERVINGS

SERVING SIZE: $1^{1}/_{2}$ cups, 240 g, 8 oz.		
Calories per serving	130	% Daily
Calories from fat	10	Value
Total Fat	1 g	2%
Saturated Fat	0 g	0%
Cholesterol	0 mg	0%
Sodium	320 mg	13%
Total Carbohydrates	25 g	8%
Sugars	4 g	
Dietary Fiber	6 g	25%
Protein	6 g	
Vitamin A		107%
Vitamin C		20%
Calcium		9%
Iron		17%
Carbohydrate Choice	**$1^{1}/_{2}$**	

EXCHANGES: 3 Vegetable, $1/2$ Fat, $1/2$ Starch

PREPARATION

1. In a large stockpot, heat the oil over medium heat, add the onions and sauté for 5-7 minutes until translucent.

2. Add the celeriac, celery, zucchini, carrots, red bell peppers, white beans, tomatoes and water and cook for $1^{1}/_{2}$ hours, until the beans are soft.

3. Add the salt, pepper and parsley, cook for an additional 5 minutes and then serve.

✳ Soup may be stored in an airtight container in the refrigerator for up to 4 days.

¤ *Minestrone Soup*

BEET & TURNIP SOUP WITH SEMOLINA BALLS

The vegetables in this soup are filled with iron and provide nearly half the amount of the recommended daily intake! This soup gets even better after being refrigerated overnight, so make it the day before guests arrive and you'll have a hearty first course already prepared.

INGREDIENTS

1 yellow onion, coarsely chopped

1 large turnip, peeled, halved and sliced into $1/4$-inch slices

1 large beet, peeled, halved and sliced into $1/4$-inch slices

2 celery ribs, coarsely chopped

$1/2$ cup parsley, coarsely chopped

$1/2$ cup cilantro, coarsely chopped

3 cups Swiss chard, coarsely chopped

5 cups strained Chicken Broth (see page 25) or strained Vegetable Broth (see page 31)

5 cups water

3 tablespoons tomato paste

3 garlic cloves, minced

1 teaspoon salt

Freshly ground pepper

1 teaspoon sugar substitute

$1/2$ cup fresh lemon juice

Whole-wheat Semolina Balls (see page 40)

10 SERVINGS

SERVING SIZE: 1$1/2$ cups, 210 g, 7 oz.

Calories per serving	70	% Daily
Calories from fat	10	Value
Total Fat	1 g	2%
Saturated Fat	0 g	0%
Cholesterol	10 mg	3%
Sodium	275 mg	11%
Total Carbohydrates	10 g	3%
Sugars	4 g	
Dietary Fiber	3 g	12%
Protein	4 g	
Vitamin A		33%
Vitamin C		35%
Calcium		7%
Iron		10%

Carbohydrate Choice $1/2$

EXCHANGES: 2 Vegetable, $1/2$ Fat

PREPARATION

1. Spray a large stockpot with cooking oil, place over medium heat and add the onions. Sauté for about 5-7 minutes, until translucent.

2. Add the turnips, beet, celery, parsley, cilantro, Swiss chard, chicken or vegetable broth, and water. Increase heat and bring to a boil. Reduce heat to medium and cook for about 1 hour, until vegetables are tender.

3. Add the tomato paste, garlic, salt, and pepper and cook for an additional 10 minutes.

4. Stir in the sugar substitute and lemon juice and add the semolina balls (recipe on page 40) and cook for 10-15 minutes before serving.

✱ Soup may be stored in an airtight container in the refrigerator for up to 4 days.

¤ *Beet & Turnip Soup with Semolina Balls*

WHOLE-WHEAT SEMOLINA BALLS

Cook these lightly spiced balls in Beet & Turnip Soup (see page 38) for a flavorful meal.

INGREDIENTS

1 1/2 cups whole-wheat semolina
3/4 cup water
1/2 teaspoon paprika
1/2 teaspoon cumin

10 SERVINGS

SERVING SIZE: 1 1/2 cups soup + 3 semolina balls, 240 g, 8 oz.

		% Daily Value
Calories per serving	140	
Calories from fat	10	
Total Fat	1 g	2%
Saturated Fat	0 g	0%
Cholesterol	10 mg	3%
Sodium	360 mg	15%
Total Carbohydrates	25 g	8%
Sugars	4 g	
Dietary Fiber	3 g	12%
Protein	6 g	
Vitamin A		30%
Vitamin C		35%
Calcium		7%
Iron		11%
Carbohydrate Choice	**1 1/2**	

EXCHANGES: 2 Vegetable, 1/2 Fat, 1 Starch

PREPARATION

1. In a large bowl, mix together all of the ingredients and allow mixture to rest for 10 minutes.

2. Knead the mixture for 3-5 minutes.

3. Using a teaspoon, scoop out the mixture and roll into a ball using your hands. Repeat with the remaining mixture.

4. Use the back of the teaspoon to flatten each of the balls.

5. Add to soup and cook for 10-15 minutes before serving.

* Balls may be stored in an airtight container in the refrigerator for up to 4 days.

CARROT & LENTIL SOUP

The carrots give this soup its beautiful rich orange color and provide nearly double the daily recommended amount of vitamin A.

INGREDIENTS

1 tablespoon olive oil
1 yellow onion, chopped
2 garlic cloves, minced
2 tomatoes, chopped
3 cups water
4 carrots, peeled and sliced
$^1/_2$ cup yellow lentils
$^1/_2$ cup parsley, chopped
1 tablespoon white vinegar
1 teaspoon salt
Freshly ground pepper

For garnish:
$^1/_2$ cup parsley, finely chopped

6 SERVINGS

SERVING SIZE: 1 cup, 210 g, 7 oz.		
Calories per serving	100	% Daily
Calories from fat	20	Value
Total Fat	2 g	4%
Saturated Fat	0 g	0%
Cholesterol	0 mg	0%
Sodium	680 mg	28%
Total Carbohydrates	17 g	6%
Sugars	4 g	
Dietary Fiber	4 g	16%
Protein	5 g	
Vitamin A		168%
Vitamin C		18%
Calcium		4%
Iron		11%
Carbohydrate Choice	1	
EXCHANGES: 2 Vegetable, $^1/_2$ Starch		

PREPARATION

1. Heat the olive oil in a large stockpot over medium heat and add the onions. Sauté for about 7 minutes, until onions are translucent. Add the garlic and continue to sauté another 2 minutes. Add the tomatoes and cook for an additional 3 minutes.

2. Add the water, carrots, lentils and parsley, cover and cook for 20 minutes on low heat.

3. Use an immersion blender to blend the soup until smooth.

4. Add the vinegar, salt and pepper and cook, uncovered, for 10 minutes.

5. Garnish with parsley and serve.

* Soup may be stored in an airtight container in the refrigerator for up to 5 days.

APPETIZERS, DIPS & BAKED GOODS

OLIVE & PUMPKIN SEED SPELT ROLLS

Spelt flour is considered a more healthy option for baking, as a replacement for all-purpose flour. Spelt flour is as easy to work as regular flour and the taste is not compromised.

15 ROLLS

SERVING SIZE: 1 roll, 30 g, 1 oz.

| Calories per serving | 70 | % Daily |
Calories from fat	20	Value
Total Fat	2 g	3%
Saturated Fat	0 g	0%
Cholesterol	0 mg	0%
Sodium	140 mg	6%
Total Carbohydrates	13 g	4%
Sugars	1 g	
Dietary Fiber	3 g	12%
Protein	3 g	
Vitamin A		0%
Vitamin C		0%
Calcium		1%
Iron		1%

Carbohydrate Choice 1

EXCHANGES: 1 Starch

INGREDIENTS

- 1/3 cup reduced fat (2%) milk, lukewarm
- 1 tablespoon olive oil
- 1 teaspoon active dry yeast
- 2 cups spelt flour
- 2 tablespoons wheat bran
- 1/2 cup all-purpose flour
- 1/2 teaspoon salt
- 1 cup green olives, pitted and chopped
- 2 teaspoons fresh rosemary leaves
- 1/2 cup water, at room temperature
- 1 egg, beaten
- 1 1/2 tablespoons pumpkin seeds

PREPARATION

1. In a small bowl, mix together the milk and olive oil. Add the dry yeast and 2 tablespoons of the spelt flour and mix until smooth. Allow it to stand for 10 minutes at room temperature, until small bubbles form on surface.

2. Meanwhile, in a separate bowl, mix together the remaining spelt flour, wheat bran, all-purpose flour, salt, olives and 1 teaspoon of the rosemary leaves.

3. Using a mixer fitted with a hook attachment, pour the yeast mixture into the flour mixture, add the water and mix on medium speed for about 5 minutes, until dough is formed. If the dough is too dry, add some water. If it is too sticky, add some flour.

4. Cover the bowl with a damp kitchen towel, and allow dough to rise in a warm place for about 1 hour, until it doubles in size.

5. Divide the dough into 15 equal pieces, 1 oz. each. Shape each piece into a ball, the size of a ping pong ball. Place the rolls, 1 inch apart, on a baking sheet lined with parchment paper. Brush each roll with the beaten egg and evenly sprinkle on the remaining rosemary leaves and pumpkin seeds.

6. Allow the rolls to rise in a warm place for about 40 minutes, until they double in volume.

7. Preheat oven to 400ºF and bake for 15-17 minutes, until golden and firm to the touch.

✳ Rolls may be stored in an airtight container in the freezer for up to 1 month.

¤ *Olive & Pumpkin Seed Spelt Rolls*

YOGURT-SPINACH SCONES

Spinach has a very high nutritional value and is extremely rich in antioxidants, vitamins and minerals, such as vitamin A, vitamin C, magnesium, iron, calcium and folic acid. These scones are a great snack to serve with brunch.

INGREDIENTS

2 cups whole-wheat flour

1 tablespoon baking powder

1^1/$_2$ cups low-fat plain yogurt

4 tablespoons canola oil

1^1/$_2$ cups fresh spinach leaves, cooked and drained

15 SCONES

SERVING SIZE: 1 scone, 35 g, about 1 oz.

Calories per serving	80	% Daily
Calories from fat	30	Value
Total Fat	3 g	5%
Saturated Fat	0 g	0%
Cholesterol	0 mg	0%
Sodium	120 mg	5%
Total Carbohydrates	12 g	4%
Sugars	1 g	
Dietary Fiber	2 g	8%
Protein	2 g	
Vitamin A		5%
Vitamin C		2%
Calcium		3%
Iron		1%

Carbohydrate Choice   1

EXCHANGES: ^{1}/$_2$ Starch, 1 Vegetable

PREPARATION

1. Preheat oven to 350ºF. Spray a muffin pan with cooking oil.

2. In a large bowl, mix together the flour, baking powder and yogurt.

3. Add the oil and spinach and mix until all ingredients are combined and dough is formed.

4. Divide the dough into 15 equal pieces and with slightly wet hands, roll each piece into a ball, slightly larger than the size of a ping pong ball. Place the rolls into the prepared muffin pan.

5. Bake for 15-17 minutes until golden and firm to the touch. Serve warm.

✳ Scones may be stored in an airtight container in the freezer for up to 1 month.

MUSHROOM SCONES

Mushrooms contain about 80% to 90% water and are very low in calories. They have very little sodium and fat. Hence, they are an ideal food for people following a weight management program or those on a diet to control hypertension. They are a good source of potassium, which helps control blood pressure, as well as riboflavin, niacin and selenium.

INGREDIENTS

2 tablespoons canola oil
1 yellow onion, finely chopped
2 garlic cloves, minced
2 cups white mushrooms, coarsely chopped
2 cups whole-wheat flour
1 teaspoon salt
1 tablespoon baking powder
1½ cups low-fat plain yogurt

15 SCONES

SERVING SIZE: 1 scone, 35 g, about 1 oz.

		% Daily Value
Calories per serving	60	
Calories from fat	10	
Total Fat	1 g	2%
Saturated Fat	0 g	0%
Cholesterol	0 mg	0%
Sodium	145 mg	6%
Total Carbohydrates	11 g	4%
Sugars	2 g	
Dietary Fiber	2 g	8%
Protein	2 g	
Vitamin A		0%
Vitamin C		2%
Calcium		11%
Iron		4%
Carbohydrate Choice	1	

EXCHANGES: ½ Vegetable, ½ Starch

PREPARATION

1. Heat the oil in a skillet over medium heat and sauté the onions for about 5-7 minutes, until golden. Add the garlic and mushrooms and continue to sauté for another 5-7 minutes, until mushrooms are tender. Remove from heat.

2. Preheat oven to 350ºF. Spray a muffin pan with cooking oil.

3. In a large bowl, mix together the flour, salt, baking powder, yogurt and mushroom mixture.

4. Divide the dough into 15 equal pieces and with slightly wet hands, roll each piece into a ball, slightly larger than the size of a ping pong ball. Place the rolls into the prepared muffin pan.

5. Bake for 15-17 minutes until golden and firm to the touch. Serve warm.

✳ Scones may be stored in an airtight container in the freezer for up to 1 month.

ONION & THYME OAT MUFFINS

These muffins supply fiber with the whole-wheat flour, oats and oat bran. The flavor of the onions blends well with the subtle thyme flavor.

INGREDIENTS

1 tablespoon olive oil
1 small yellow onion, finely chopped
1/2 teaspoon dried thyme leaves
1 egg
1 cup reduced-fat (2%) milk
1 teaspoon salt
1/4 cup water
1 1/2 cups whole-wheat flour
1/2 cup old-fashioned oats
2 tablespoons oat bran
1 tablespoon baking powder

12 MUFFINS

SERVING SIZE: 1 muffin, 50 g, 1 1/2 oz.

		% Daily Value
Calories per serving	100	
Calories from fat	20	
Total Fat	2 g	4%
Saturated Fat	1 g	3%
Cholesterol	25 mg	8%
Sodium	375 mg	16%
Total Carbohydrates	16 g	5%
Sugars	1 g	
Dietary Fiber	2 g	8%
Protein	4 g	
Vitamin A		1%
Vitamin C		0%
Calcium		5%
Iron		5%

Carbohydrate Choice   1

EXCHANGES: 1 Starch, 1/2 Vegetable

PREPARATION

1. Heat the olive oil in a skillet over medium heat and sauté the onion for about 5-7 minutes, until golden. Add the thyme leaves and remove from heat.

2. Preheat oven to 400°F. Spray a muffin pan with cooking oil.

3. In a bowl, whisk together the egg, milk, salt and water. Add the sautéed onion mixture.

4. In a separate bowl, mix together the flour, oats, oat bran and baking powder. Using a rubber spatula, fold the flour mixture into the egg mixture until all ingredients are combined.

5. Spoon the batter into the prepared muffin pan, filling each cup 3/4 full. Bake for 10-15 minutes, until golden. Cool on a wire rack for 10 minutes until slightly cooled and serve.

✽ Muffins may be stored in an airtight container in the freezer for up to 1 month.

BAKED SUN-DRIED TOMATO ENGLISH BRAN MUFFINS

These muffins are very similar in taste to English muffins. I recommend making the dough for these muffins the night before and refrigerating it. Allow the dough to reach room temperature before baking.

12 MUFFINS

SERVING SIZE: 1 muffin, 45 g, 1¹/₂ oz.

		% Daily
Calories per serving	90	Value
Calories from fat	10	
Total Fat	1 g	2%
Saturated Fat	0 g	0%
Cholesterol	0 mg	0%
Sodium	150 mg	6%
Total Carbohydrates	18 g	6%
Sugars	1 g	
Dietary Fiber	2 g	8%
Protein	3 g	
Vitamin A		0%
Vitamin C		1%
Calcium		3%
Iron		7%

Carbohydrate Choice 1

EXCHANGES: 1 Starch, ¹/₂ Vegetable

INGREDIENTS

1 teaspoon honey
2 tablespoons + ¹/₂ cup warm water
1¹/₂ teaspoons active dry yeast
3 tablespoons sun-dried tomatoes, finely chopped
1 cup all-purpose flour
1 cup whole-wheat flour
¹/₄ cup wheat bran
1 cup low-fat plain yogurt
¹/₂ teaspoon salt
¹/₂ teaspoon baking soda

PREPARATION

1. In a small bowl, mix together the honey and 2 tablespoons of warm water. Add the dry yeast and allow it to stand for about 10 minutes at room temperature, until yeast is foamy.

2. In a separate bowl, mix together the remaining ¹/₂ cup warm water with the sun-dried tomatoes.

3. Using a mixer fitted with a hook attachment, add the yeast mixture, all-purpose flour, whole-wheat flour, wheat bran, yogurt, salt and baking soda and mix on low speed for 3 minutes.

4. Add the sun-dried tomatoes and water to the flour mixture and mix for an additional 3 minutes, until dough is formed.

5. Cover bowl with a damp kitchen towel and allow dough to rise in a warm place for about 1 hour, until it doubles in size.

6. Preheat oven to 400ºF. Spray a muffin pan with cooking oil.

7. Evenly spoon dough into the prepared muffin pan.

8. Bake for 15 minutes, until golden and firm to the touch. Serve warm.

＊ Muffins may be stored in an airtight container in the freezer for up to 1 month.

TUNA SALAD WRAPS

Canned tuna is not only high in protein and vitamin D, but also a good source of omega-3 fatty acids, making it a healthy choice for a quick and easy lunch.

INGREDIENTS

2 cans tuna in water, drained
3 tablespoons light mayonnaise
1 cup Pickled Cucumbers & Dill Salad (see page 70)
1 tablespoon ketchup
1 tablespoon fresh lemon juice
20 lettuce leaves

10 SERVINGS

SERVING SIZE: 2 tablespoons, 30 g, 1 oz.		
Calories per serving	30	% Daily
Calories from fat	10	Value
Total Fat	1 g	2%
Saturated Fat	0 g	0%
Cholesterol	5 mg	2%
Sodium	85 mg	4%
Total Carbohydrates	0 g	0%
Sugars	0 g	
Dietary Fiber	1 g	0%
Protein	5 g	
Vitamin A		0%
Vitamin C		5%
Calcium		1%
Iron		3%
Carbohydrate Choice	0	
EXCHANGES: ½ Lean Meat		

PREPARATION

1. In a large bowl, mix all ingredients, except lettuce, until well combined.

2. Spoon 1 tablespoon tuna salad onto a lettuce leaf and roll up. Secure with a toothpick and serve.

✳ Salad may be stored in an airtight container in the refrigerator for up to 2 days.

CUCUMBER RAITA

This dip is inspired by Indian cuisine. You can find garam masala in the spice section of your local supermarket. It is refreshing, low in calories and is perfect when served with the scones in this chapter.

INGREDIENTS

2 large cucumbers, thinly sliced
2 cups low-fat plain yogurt
$1/4$ cup parsley, finely chopped
$1/4$ cup mint leaves, finely chopped
1 teaspoon garam masala or curry powder
$1/2$ teaspoon caraway seeds
$1/2$ teaspoon cayenne pepper (optional)

For garnish:
Mint leaves
Caraway seeds

8 SERVINGS

SERVING SIZE: 1 cup, 150 g, 5 oz.

		% Daily Value
Calories per serving	60	
Calories from fat	10	
Total Fat	1 g	2%
Saturated Fat	1 g	4%
Cholesterol	5 mg	2%
Sodium	50 mg	2%
Total Carbohydrates	7 g	2%
Sugars	5 g	
Dietary Fiber	1 g	4%
Protein	4 g	
Vitamin A		8%
Vitamin C		18%
Calcium		14%
Iron		1%
Carbohydrate Choice	$1/2$	

EXCHANGES: $1/2$ **Vegetable,**
$1/2$ **Low-Fat Milk**

PREPARATION

1. Place all ingredients in a large bowl, mix until well combined.

2. Garnish with mint leaves and caraway seeds and serve.

¤ *Cucumber Raita*

AVOCADO DIP

This is a very easy dip to make and it goes really well with both of the scone recipes in this chapter. Even though this recipe contains almost no carbohydrates, it still has a relatively high amount of fat.
This dip should be eaten soon after preparation, as it will only last a few hours in the refrigerator.

INGREDIENTS

3 medium-sized ripe avocados
1¹/₂ cups green onion, white and green parts, thinly sliced
4 tablespoons fresh lemon juice
¹/₄ teaspoon salt
Freshly ground pepper

For garnish:
1 tablespoon green onion, white and green parts, thinly sliced

20 SERVINGS

SERVING SIZE: 2 tablespoons, 30 g, 1 oz.		
Calories per serving	60	% Daily
Calories from fat	30	Value
Total Fat	4 g	6%
Saturated Fat	1 g	4%
Cholesterol	0 mg	0%
Sodium	40 mg	2%
Total Carbohydrates	2 g	0%
Sugars	0 g	
Dietary Fiber	2 g	8%
Protein	1 g	
Vitamin A		2%
Vitamin C		5%
Calcium		1%
Iron		2%
Carbohydrate Choice 0		
EXCHANGES: 1 Fat, ¹/₂ Vegetable		

PREPARATION

1. Slice each avocado in half, remove the seed and use a tablespoon to scoop out the avocado flesh from the peel. Place in a mixing bowl and mash with a fork.

2. Add all remaining ingredients to bowl and mix until combined.

3. Garnish with green onion and serve.

STUFFED BELL PEPPERS

This recipe is easy to make and packed with vitamin C, making it a great option for an easy lunch.

INGREDIENTS

14 oz. white mushrooms
2 garlic cloves
1 teaspoon Thai red curry paste
4 1/2 teaspoons low-sodium soy sauce
1 egg
2 yellow bell peppers, halved horizontally, seeds removed

4 SERVINGS

SERVING SIZE: 1/2 **pepper, 180 g, 6 oz.**

		% Daily
Calories per serving	70	Value
Calories from fat	20	
Total Fat	2 g	3%
Saturated Fat	0 g	0%
Cholesterol	75 mg	25%
Sodium	210 mg	9%
Total Carbohydrates	11 g	4%
Sugars	2 g	
Dietary Fiber	2 g	8%
Protein	5 g	
Vitamin A		6%
Vitamin C		200%
Calcium		2%
Iron		7%

Carbohydrate Choice 1/2

EXCHANGES: 2 Vegetable, 1/2 **Lean Meat**

PREPARATION

1. Place the mushrooms and garlic in a food processor and pulse several times until blended. Place mixture in a large bowl.

2. Add all remaining ingredients, excluding the peppers, and mix until all ingredients are combined.

3. Place a piece of parchment paper on the bottom half of a large bamboo steamer. Place the pepper halves onto the parchment paper and fill each one with the mushroom mixture.

4. Close steamer and cook over boiling water for 15-20 minutes until the peppers are tender and serve.

✳ Peppers may be stored in an airtight container in the refrigerator for 2 days.

¤ *Vietnamese Eggrolls*

VIETNAMESE EGGROLLS

This is a really easy recipe to make once you have all the ingredients on hand. The vegetables in this dish provide a great source of vitamin A.

INGREDIENTS

1 oz. cellophane noodles
Six 10-inch rice paper sheets
1 carrot, peeled and julienned
1 cup cabbage, thinly sliced
1 cup bean sprouts
2 tablespoons low-sodium soy sauce
2 tablespoons roasted peanuts, chopped
Sweet Chili Sauce (see page 58)

6 SERVINGS

SERVING SIZE: 1 roll + chili sauce, 120 g, 4 oz.

Calories per serving	130	% Daily
Calories from fat	20	Value
Total Fat	2 g	3%
Saturated Fat	0 g	0%
Cholesterol	0 mg	0%
Sodium	230 mg	10%
Total Carbohydrates	23 g	8%
Sugars	1 g	
Dietary Fiber	2 g	8%
Protein	4 g	
Vitamin A		74%
Vitamin C		62%
Calcium		3%
Iron		4%
Carbohydrate Choice	1½	

EXCHANGES: 2 Vegetable , 1 Starch

PREPARATION

1. Soak noodles in hot water for 10 minutes, or until soft, and then drain, retaining the cooking water.

2. Working quickly, dip a rice paper sheet into the warm water, making sure all parts of the paper are wet. Place on a clean work surface.

3. On the lower edge of the rice paper, closest to you, place 1 tablespoon each of carrots, cabbage, bean sprouts and noodles, leaving 1 inch on the edge. Evenly pour 1 teaspoon of soy sauce and sprinkle 1 teaspoon of chopped peanuts over the vegetables.

4. Begin to fold egg roll like an envelope: first, fold over the lower 1-inch edge over the filling, then the left edge, and then the right edge. Now roll the roll up to the top edge. Place the wrapped egg roll on a serving plate and continue with the remaining rice paper.

5. Cut each eggroll in half, and serve with Sweet Chili Sauce (see page 58).

SWEET CHILI SAUCE

This recipe contains almost no sugar, whereas the store-bought version is high in sugar and therefore in calories. This sauce gets spicier with time, so take into consideration that the longer it sits in the refrigerator, the spicier it becomes.

INGREDIENTS

2 red bell peppers, cut into 1-inch cubes
1 dried red chili pepper
1 teaspoon sugar substitute
1 tablespoon white vinegar
2 garlic cloves
$1/2$ teaspoon salt

6 SERVINGS

SERVING SIZE: 3 tablespoons, 60 g, 2 oz.

		% Daily Value
Calories per serving	20	
Calories from fat	0	
Total Fat	0 g	0%
Saturated Fat	0 g	0%
Cholesterol	0 mg	0%
Sodium	170 mg	7%
Total Carbohydrates	4 g	1%
Sugars	3 g	
Dietary Fiber	1 g	4%
Protein	1 g	
Vitamin A		32%
Vitamin C		100%
Calcium		2%
Iron		3%
Carbohydrate Choice	0	
EXCHANGES: 1 Vegetable		

PREPARATION

1. Steam the bell peppers until slightly softened.

2. Place all ingredients in a food processor and blend until all ingredients are combined.

✴ Sauce may be stored in an airtight container in the refrigerator for up to 2 weeks.

WALNUT PESTO

This pesto contains less than two-thirds the amount of calories found in traditional pesto recipes. This pesto does not contain any Parmesan cheese, uses a small amount of olive oil and is made mostly from walnuts. Walnuts are a great source of unsaturated fats, contain a large amount of omega-3 and are high in magnesium. The lemon juice in this recipe keeps the pesto from turning brown, and it is a good idea to add a little more before serving if the pesto has been stored in the refrigerator.

10 SERVINGS

SERVING SIZE: 1 tablespoon, 15 g, ¹/₂ oz.		
Calories per serving	40	% Daily
Calories from fat	40	Value
Total Fat	4 g	6%
Saturated Fat	0 g	0%
Cholesterol	0 mg	0%
Sodium	195 mg	8%
Total Carbohydrates	1 g	0%
Sugars	0 g	
Dietary Fiber	1 g	0%
Protein	1 g	
Vitamin A		8%
Vitamin C		3%
Calcium		1%
Iron		2%
Carbohydrate Choice	0	
EXCHANGES: 1 Fat		

INGREDIENTS

4 tablespoons walnuts
2 cups basil leaves
1 garlic clove
2 tablespoons olive oil
1 teaspoon salt
2 tablespoons water
2 tablespoons fresh lemon juice

PREPARATION

1. Place all ingredients in a food processor and blend until all ingredients are combined.

2. Store in a non-metal airtight container to prevent discoloring.

✳ Pesto may be stored in an airtight container in the freezer for up to 2 months.

MEXICAN-STYLE EGGS

Although this recipe contains the entire recommended daily intake of cholesterol, it is filled with vegetables which contain fiber, minerals and lycopene. Served with a slice of whole-wheat bread, this recipe becomes a hearty meal.

INGREDIENTS

1 tablespoon olive oil
1 yellow onion, finely chopped
1 red bell pepper, cut into $1/2$-inch cubes
4 ripe tomatoes, coarsely chopped
1 tablespoon tomato paste
1 cup cooked white beans
1 cup cilantro, finely chopped
$1/2$ teaspoon salt
Freshly ground pepper
4 eggs

4 SERVINGS

SERVING SIZE: 1 egg + 1 cup sauce, 210 g, 7 oz.		
Calories per serving	190	% Daily
Calories from fat	70	Value
Total Fat	8 g	13%
Saturated Fat	2 g	8%
Cholesterol	300 mg	100%
Sodium	310 mg	13%
Total Carbohydrates	18 g	6%
Sugars	5 g	
Dietary Fiber	4 g	16%
Protein	13 g	
Vitamin A		46%
Vitamin C		70%
Calcium		10%
Iron		18%
Carbohydrate Choice	1	

EXCHANGES: 2 Vegetable, $1/2$ Starch, $1/2$ Fat, 1 Medium-Fat Meat

PREPARATION

1. In a large skillet, heat the olive oil over medium heat and add the onion. Sauté for about 5 minutes, until golden. Add the red pepper and sauté for another 2 minutes. Add the tomatoes and continue cooking for another 10 minutes.

2. Add the tomato paste, beans and cilantro and stir until all ingredients are combined. Season with salt and pepper and continue cooking for an additional 5 minutes.

3. Carefully break the eggs into the sauce and cook to the desired degree of doneness. Serve warm.

¤ *Chicken & Avocado Tortilla Wraps*

CHICKEN & AVOCADO TORTILLA WRAPS

This recipe is a great lunch option, especially when served with a side salad. Corn tortillas have fewer calories than flour tortillas and are therefore recommended. You can use purchased tortillas or make your own from the recipe on page 64.

INGREDIENTS

10 oz. boneless skinless chicken breasts, cut into strips
9 tablespoons Sweet Chili Sauce (see page 58)
3 corn tortillas (purchased or see page 64)
6 tablespoons Walnut Pesto (see page 59)
6 outer leaves romaine lettuce, chopped
1 medium-sized avocado, peeled, seeded and thinly sliced
1 red bell pepper, thinly sliced

6 SERVINGS

SERVING SIZE: 1/2 filled tortilla, 150 g, 5 oz.

Calories per serving	210	% Daily
Calories from fat	80	Value
Total Fat	9 g	14%
Saturated Fat	1 g	5%
Cholesterol	35 mg	12%
Sodium	185 mg	8%
Total Carbohydrates	16 g	5%
Sugars	1 g	
Dietary Fiber	3 g	12%
Protein	16 g	
Vitamin A		10%
Vitamin C		64%
Calcium		4%
Iron		12%

Carbohydrate Choice   1

EXCHANGES: 1 1/2 Vegetable, 1 1/2 Fat, 1/2 Starch, 1 1/2 Lean Meat

PREPARATION

1. Place chicken breast strips in a bowl with the Sweet Chili Sauce and allow them to marinate for 10 minutes.

2. In a large nonstick skillet, sauté the chicken until completely cooked through. Remove from heat.

3. Place a tortilla on a clean working surface and spread on 1 tablespoon of pesto.

4. On the lower edge of the tortilla, closest to you, place lettuce, avocado, bell pepper and chicken onto the pesto.

5. Roll up to the top edge. Place the wrapped tortilla on a serving plate and continue preparing the remaining tortillas.

6. Cut each tortilla in half and serve.

HOMEMADE CORN TORTILLAS

Use these freshly made tortillas to serve your favorite sautéed vegtables.

INGREDIENTS

2 cups cornmeal

1 cup all-purpose flour

1 teaspoon canola oil

1$^1/_4$ cups warm water

10 SERVINGS

SERVING SIZE: 1 tortilla, 60 g, 2 oz.

Calories per serving	140	% Daily
Calories from fat	10	Value
Total Fat	1 g	2%
Saturated Fat	0 g	0%
Cholesterol	0 mg	0%
Sodium	0 mg	0%
Total Carbohydrates	29 g	10%
Sugars	1 g	
Dietary Fiber	1 g	4%
Protein	3 g	
Vitamin A		1%
Vitamin C		0%
Calcium		0%
Iron		4%

Carbohydrate Choice   2

EXCHANGES: 2 Starch

PREPARATION

1. In a large bowl, mix together the cornmeal and flour. Add the oil and $^1/_4$ cup of the water and begin to knead with your hands.

2. Continue kneading while gradually adding the remaining 1 cup water, until dough is formed, and the mixture no longer sticks to your hands. Allow the dough to rest at room temperature for 20 minutes.

3. Divide the dough into 10 equal pieces. Roll each piece into a ball, about the size of an egg.

4. Working on a floured surface, roll out each ball to about an 8-inch diameter circle. Heat a tortilla pan on high heat and cook each tortilla on each side for 2-3 minutes, until brown spots appear. Cover immediately with a damp kitchen towel to keep tortilla from drying out. Use immediately or store in an airtight container.

✷ Tortillas may be stored in an airtight container at room temperature for up to 2 days.

STUFFED MUSHROOMS

These mushrooms are the perfect finger food to serve at your next party. These taste so good that your guests won't even know that they are suited for the people following a diabetic diet.

INGREDIENTS

4 large portobello mushrooms
1 yellow onion, finely chopped
1 tablespoon olive oil
1 tablespoon butter
2 garlic cloves, minced
1 tablespoon fresh or dried thyme
$^1/_2$ cup parsley, finely chopped
1$^1/_2$ teaspoons salt
1 tablespoon whole-wheat flour
$^3/_4$ cup water
1 tablespoon bread crumbs
$^1/_4$ cup green onions, finely chopped, green part only
4 tablespoons Parmesan cheese, grated

4 SERVINGS

SERVING SIZE: 1 mushroom, 150 g, 5 oz.		
Calories per serving	120	% Daily
Calories from fat	60	Value
Total Fat	7 g	11%
Saturated Fat	3 g	14%
Cholesterol	15 mg	5%
Sodium	560 mg	23%
Total Carbohydrates	12 g	4%
Sugars	2 g	
Dietary Fiber	2 g	8%
Protein	5 g	
Vitamin A		0%
Vitamin C		18%
Calcium		8%
Iron		4%
Carbohydrate Choice	1	
EXCHANGES: 2$^1/_2$ Vegetable, 1 Fat		

PREPARATION

1. Preheat oven to 375°F.

2. Remove stems from mushrooms and finely chop stems. Place the mushroom caps aside for later use.

3. Heat the olive oil and butter in a deep saucepan over medium heat and add the onions. Sauté for 7-10 minutes, until golden. Add the chopped stems, garlic, thyme, parsley, and salt and continue to cook for another 5 minutes.

4. Add the flour and water and cook for an additional 5 minutes, while constantly stirring, until thickened. Remove from heat.

5. Add the bread crumbs and green onions and stir to combine.

6. Stuff the mushroom caps with the filling and place on a baking sheet lined with parchment paper. Top each mushroom with 1 tablespoon of Parmesan cheese. Bake for 15 minutes, until mushrooms are cooked and filling is golden.

SALADS

¤ *Quinoa, Sun-Dried Tomatoes & Feta Salad*

QUINOA, SUN-DRIED TOMATOES & FETA SALAD

Quinoa contains more protein than most other grains and is a great source of iron and calcium. This salad is made up of both carbohydrates and proteins, making it a great quick lunch option. If preparing this salad ahead of time, add the feta cheese just before serving.

6 SERVINGS

SERVING SIZE: 3/4 cup, 150 g, 5 oz.

		% Daily
Calories per serving	170	Value
Calories from fat	60	
Total Fat	6 g	10%
Saturated Fat	2 g	12%
Cholesterol	0 mg	0%
Sodium	435 mg	18%
Total Carbohydrates	22 g	7%
Sugars	3 g	
Dietary Fiber	3 g	12%
Protein	7 g	
Vitamin A		22%
Vitamin C		78%
Calcium		10%
Iron		11%
Carbohydrate Choice	1 1/2	

EXCHANGES: 1 Vegetable, 1/2 Fat, 1 Starch, 1/2 Medium-Fat Meat

INGREDIENTS

1 cup quinoa

2 cups water

1 teaspoon salt

2 tablespoons sun-dried tomatoes, cut into strips, soaked in hot water

1 tablespoon olive oil

2 red bell peppers, cut into small cubes

1/2 cup basil leaves, coarsely chopped

3 tablespoons fresh lemon juice

3 oz. feta cheese, crumbled

PREPARATION

1. Place the quinoa, water and 1/2 teaspoon of the salt in a medium saucepan and cook over high heat. Bring to a boil, lower heat, cover and cook for 15 minutes. Remove from heat and allow saucepan to stand, covered, for an additional 10 minutes.

2. Meanwhile, drain the sun-dried tomatoes and place them in a small bowl with the olive oil. Allow to stand at room temperature for 10 minutes.

3. In a large serving bowl, mix together the quinoa, sun-dried tomatoes (with the oil), red bell peppers, basil leaves, lemon juice and remaining 1/2 teaspoon of salt. Sprinkle with the crumbled feta cheese and serve.

✱ Quinoa, without the added cheese, may be stored in an airtight container in the refrigerator for up to 3 days.

PICKLED CUCUMBERS & DILL SALAD

This recipe is a great replacement for store-bought pickles, which contain a large amount of sodium. This guilt-free salad contains almost no calories, fat, sugar or sodium.

INGREDIENTS

4 cups cucumbers, peeled and cut into small cubes
4 tablespoons dill, finely chopped
4 tablespoons white vinegar

8 SERVINGS

SERVING SIZE: about ¹/₂ cup, 60 g, 2 oz.

| Calories per serving | 10 | % Daily |
Calories from fat	0	Value
Total Fat	0 g	0%
Saturated Fat	0 g	0%
Cholesterol	0 mg	0%
Sodium	5 mg	0%
Total Carbohydrates	3 g	1%
Sugars	1 g	
Dietary Fiber	1 g	4%
Protein	0 g	
Vitamin A		11%
Vitamin C		16%
Calcium		2%
Iron		3%

Carbohydrate Choice 0

EXCHANGES: ¹/₂ **Vegetable**

PREPARATION

1. Place all ingredients in a large bowl and mix. Allow to stand for 30 minutes at room temperature.

2. Drain the liquid from the salad and serve.

✳ Salad may be stored in an airtight container in the refrigerator for up to 3 days.

APPLE
&
MINT
SAMBAL

A sambal is a relish found in Indonesian cuisine. It may be eaten on its own or as a sauce with seafood or rice dishes.

INGREDIENTS

2 red apples, unpeeled, cored and cut into $1/2$-inch cubes
$1/2$ cup mint leaves, coarsely chopped
1 red bell pepper, cut into $1/2$-inch cubes
$1/4$ cup fresh lemon juice

For garnish:
1 tablespoon peanuts, finely chopped

5 SERVINGS

PREPARATION

1. Place all salad ingredients in a medium serving bowl and mix well.

2. Garnish with peanuts and serve.

SERVING SIZE: 1 cup, 100 g, 3$1/2$ oz.

		% Daily Value
Calories per serving	50	
Calories from fat	10	
Total Fat	1 g	2%
Saturated Fat	0 g	0%
Cholesterol	0 mg	0%
Sodium	5 mg	0%
Total Carbohydrates	9 g	3%
Sugars	7 g	
Dietary Fiber	3 g	12%
Protein	2 g	
Vitamin A		26%
Vitamin C		75%
Calcium		2%
Iron		3%
Carbohydrate Choice	$1/2$	

EXCHANGES: $1/2$ Vegetable, $1/2$ Fruit

¤ *Beet, Carrot & Apple Salad*

BEET, CARROT & APPLE SALAD

This is a great salad to serve alongside a beef or chicken dish. The fat in this salad is derived solely from the walnuts and olive oil, both of which are important sources of omega-3.

INGREDIENTS

1 medium-sized beet, cooked, peeled and julienned
2 carrots, peeled and julienned
3 Granny Smith apples, unpeeled, cored and thinly sliced
$^1/_2$ cup walnuts, coarsely chopped

For the dressing:
1 tablespoon Dijon mustard
$^1/_3$ cup fresh lemon juice
1 teaspoon honey
1 tablespoon olive oil

8 SERVINGS

SERVING SIZE: 1 cup, 100 g, 3$^1/_2$ oz.

		% Daily Value
Calories per serving	90	
Calories from fat	40	
Total Fat	4 g	6%
Saturated Fat	0 g	0%
Cholesterol	0 mg	0%
Sodium	50 mg	2%
Total Carbohydrates	13 g	4%
Sugars	2 g	
Dietary Fiber	2 g	8%
Protein	1 g	
Vitamin A		83%
Vitamin C		9%
Calcium		2%
Iron		4%
Carbohydrate Choice	1	
EXCHANGES: 1 Vegetable, 1 Fat, $^1/_2$ Fruit		

PREPARATION

1. Place all the salad ingredients in a large mixing bowl.

2. In a small bowl, whisk together all of the dressing ingredients until smooth.

3. Drizzle the dressing over the salad, toss and serve.

* Salad may be stored in an airtight container in the refrigerator for up to 3 days.

INDONESIAN SHRIMP & BANANA SALAD

This is a festive salad, great to serve as part of a holiday buffet.

INGREDIENTS

$^1/_2$ cup white basmati rice

1 cup water

1 tablespoon fresh lemon juice

1 tablespoon olive oil

2 celery ribs, thinly sliced

$^1/_2$ pound iceberg lettuce, leaves torn

4 bananas, peeled and sliced into $^1/_4$-inch slices

2 cups cherry tomatoes, halved

15 oz. shrimp, fresh or frozen, cooked, peeled, deveined and chilled

For the dressing:

1 tablespoon olive oil

2 tablespoons fresh lemon juice

Pinch of cayenne pepper

For serving:

$^1/_2$ cup Cocktail Sauce (see page 75)

10 SERVINGS

SERVING SIZE: 1$^1/_2$ cups, 150 g, 5 oz.

		% Daily Value
Calories per serving	120	
Calories from fat	30	
Total Fat	3 g	5%
Saturated Fat	0 g	0%
Cholesterol	55 mg	18%
Sodium	70 mg	3%
Total Carbohydrates	16 g	5%
Sugars	5 g	
Dietary Fiber	2 g	8%
Protein	9 g	
Vitamin A		3%
Vitamin C		14%
Calcium		3%
Iron		6%

Carbohydrate Choice 1

EXCHANGES: $^1/_2$ Starch, 1 Lean Meat, $^1/_2$ Fruit

PREPARATION

1. Place the basmati rice and water in a medium saucepan over high heat. Bring to a boil, lower heat, cover and cook for 10 minutes. Remove from heat, keep covered and allow rice to stand for another 10 minutes.

2. Add the lemon juice, olive oil and celery to the rice and mix. Pack rice in a slightly wet bowl and turn upside down onto a large serving plate.

3. Arrange the lettuce around the rice. Evenly place the banana slices and cherry tomatoes on the lettuce, and place the shrimp on top.

4. In a small bowl, mix together all of the dressing ingredients and drizzle onto the shrimp.

5. Serve with the Cocktail Sauce (traditionally served in a small bowl pressed into the middle of the rice).

COCKTAIL SAUCE

This sauce has less fat than the store-bought version and most importantly, does not contain any ketchup, which contains sugar.

INGREDIENTS

4 tablespoons light mayonnaise
2 tablespoons fresh lemon juice
2 tablespoons tomato paste
2 tablespoons dry red wine

10 SERVINGS

SERVING SIZE: 1¹/₂ tablespoons, 20 g, ²/₃ oz.

		% Daily Value
Calories per serving	30	
Calories from fat	20	
Total Fat	2 g	4%
Saturated Fat	0 g	0%
Cholesterol	0 mg	0%
Sodium	85 mg	4%
Total Carbohydrates	2 g	0%
Sugars	1 g	
Dietary Fiber	1 g	0%
Protein	0 g	
Vitamin A		1%
Vitamin C		5%
Calcium		0%
Iron		1%
Carbohydrate Choice	0	

EXCHANGES: ¹/₂ Vegetable, ¹/₂ Fat

PREPARATION

Place all ingredients in a medium bowl, whisk until smooth and serve. Add 2-3 tablespoons of water if the sauce is too thick.

✳ Sauce may be stored in an airtight container in the refrigerator for up to 1 month.

CABBAGE & CARROT SALAD

Cabbage belongs to the brassicaceae family, known for its cancer-fighting properties, while carrots are an amazing source of vitamin A. This salad is also high in vitamin C, making this recipe a great choice when you're in need of a vitamin-packed meal.

INGREDIENTS

$^1/_3$ cup freshly squeezed orange juice
$^1/_2$ cup light mayonnaise
5 tablespoons apple cider vinegar
1 teaspoon sugar substitute
2 tablespoons water
8 cups red cabbage, thinly sliced
6 carrots, peeled and julienned
1 cup green onions, green parts only, thinly sliced

For garnish:
1 tablespoon black sesame seeds

10 SERVINGS

SERVING SIZE: 1$^1/_2$ cups, 150 g, 5 oz

		% Daily Value
Calories per serving	70	
Calories from fat	30	
Total Fat	3 g	5%
Saturated Fat	0 g	0%
Cholesterol	0 mg	0%
Sodium	120 mg	5%
Total Carbohydrates	10 g	3%
Sugars	3 g	
Dietary Fiber	4 g	16%
Protein	2 g	
Vitamin A		134%
Vitamin C		50%
Calcium		7%
Iron		4%
Carbohydrate Choice	$^1/_2$	

EXCHANGES: 2 Vegetable, $^1/_2$ Fat

PREPARATION

1. In a medium bowl, whisk together the orange juice, mayonnaise, vinegar, sugar substitute and water.

2. Place the cabbage, carrots and green onion in a large serving bowl. Drizzle the dressing over salad and toss. Garnish with sesame seeds and serve.

✻ Salad may be stored in an airtight container in the refrigerator for up to 4 days.

WALNUT & VINAIGRETTE SALAD

Walnuts assist in reducing the "bad" cholesterol and preventing heart disease. Walnuts are also a great source of alpha-linolenic acids, a type of omega-3 fatty acid. This vinaigrette is a great staple to have in your refrigerator, so make it and store it in a sealed jar to have on hand.

INGREDIENTS

1 head iceberg lettuce, chopped
8 oz. baby leaf greens
5 tablespoons walnuts

For the dressing:
4 tablespoons fresh lemon juice
1 packet sugar substitute
1 tablespoon mustard
2 tablespoons orange juice
1 tablespoon water
1 teaspoon salt
Freshly ground pepper

8 SERVINGS

SERVING SIZE: 1 cup, 120 g, 4 oz.

| Calories per serving | 80 | % Daily |
Calories from fat	60	Value
Total Fat	6 g	10%
Saturated Fat	1 g	3%
Cholesterol	0 mg	0%
Sodium	315 mg	13%
Total Carbohydrates	5 g	2%
Sugars	1 g	
Dietary Fiber	2 g	7%
Protein	2 g	
Vitamin A		109%
Vitamin C		13%
Calcium		3%
Iron		5%

Carbohydrate Choice   0

EXCHANGES: 1 Vegetable, 1 Fat

PREPARATION

1. Place the lettuce, baby leaf greens and walnuts in a large serving bowl.

2. Prepare the dressing: Place all ingredients in a mixing bowl and whisk until smooth.

3. Drizzle the dressing over the lettuce, toss and serve.

ROASTED PEPPER SALSA

This salsa is a good staple to keep in your refrigerator. It is a great snack to have on hand with raw vegetables when you need something quick and healthy.

INGREDIENTS

1 large red bell pepper
1 large green bell pepper
1 large yellow/orange bell pepper

For the dressing:
4 tablespoons white vinegar
$1/3$ cup water
3 whole black peppercorns
2 bay leaves
1 teaspoon salt

20 SERVINGS

SERVING SIZE: 2 tablespoons, 30 g, 1 oz.		
Calories per serving	10	% Daily
Calories from fat	0	Value
Total Fat	0 g	0%
Saturated Fat	0 g	0%
Cholesterol	0 mg	0%
Sodium	85 mg	4%
Total Carbohydrates	1 g	0%
Sugars	1 g	
Dietary Fiber	1 g	4%
Protein	0 g	
Vitamin A		6%
Vitamin C		54%
Calcium		1%
Iron		2%
Carbohydrate Choice	0	
EXCHANGES: $1/2$ **Vegetable**		

PREPARATION

1. Roast peppers over an open flame or in broiler, turning frequently until skins are blistered.

2. Remove skins under running water and then cut peppers in half, holding them over a bowl to catch the juice. Remove seeds and stem, then chop and put in serving dish.

3. In a small saucepan bring all of the dressing ingredients to a boil over high heat and remove from heat. Pour dressing over roasted peppers and allow salad to stand for at least 15 minutes at room temperature before serving. (It's preferable to refrigerate overnight before serving.)

✳ Salsa may be stored in an airtight container in the refrigerator for up to 2 weeks.

GRAPEFRUIT & AVOCADO SALAD

This is a salad that gets tastier with time, so prepare it a day in advance and keep it refrigerated. The citrus in the grapefruit will prevent the avocado from turning brown.

INGREDIENTS

1 medium-sized avocado, peeled and seeded
2 large pink grapefruit
2 celery ribs, thinly sliced
1 red bell pepper, cut into $1/2$-inch cubes
$1/4$ cup fresh lemon juice
4 tablespoons light mayonnaise
1 tablespoon honey
1 teaspoon salt
Freshly ground pepper

10 SERVINGS

SERVING SIZE: 1$1/2$ cups, 150 g, 5 oz.

		% Daily Value
Calories per serving	80	
Calories from fat	40	
Total Fat	4 g	6%
Saturated Fat	1 g	3%
Cholesterol	0 mg	0%
Sodium	235 mg	10%
Total Carbohydrates	8 g	3%
Sugars	4 g	
Dietary Fiber	2 g	8%
Protein	1 g	
Vitamin A		20%
Vitamin C		60%
Calcium		4%
Iron		2%
Carbohydrate Choice	$1/2$	

EXCHANGES: 1 Fat, $1/2$ Fruit

PREPARATION

1. Chop avocado into large cubes. Sprinkle with a small amount of lemon juice to prevent browning.

2. Use a large, sharp knife to slice the peel off the grapefruit, making sure to remove all the white pith. Cut between the membranes to release the grapefruit segments.

3. Place the avocado, grapefruit, celery and bell pepper in a serving bowl and mix gently, making sure not to damage the avocado.

4. In a separate bowl, whisk together the lemon juice, mayonnaise, honey, salt and pepper. Drizzle the dressing over salad and serve.

✳ Salad may be stored in an airtight container in the refrigerator for up to 3 days.

¤ *Grapefruit & Avocado Salad*

WALDORF SALAD

This is a calorie-friendly version of the classic Waldorf salad and is impressive enough to serve to guests. This salad gets better with time, so prepare it in advance and keep in the refrigerator until serving.

INGREDIENTS

2 Granny Smith apples, peeled, cored and julienned
1 large celeriac, peeled and julienned
2 celery ribs, thinly sliced
1 cup fresh pineapple chunks
3 tablespoons walnuts, coarsely chopped

For the dressing:
$^1/_2$ cup low-fat plain yogurt
2 tablespoons light mayonnaise
2 packets sugar substitute
$^1/_2$ cup fresh lemon juice

10 SERVINGS

SERVING SIZE: 1 cup, 120 g, 4 oz.

		% Daily
Calories per serving	80	Value
Calories from fat	30	
Total Fat	3 g	5%
Saturated Fat	0 g	0%
Cholesterol	0 mg	0%
Sodium	80 mg	3%
Total Carbohydrates	12 g	4%
Sugars	7 g	
Dietary Fiber	1 g	4%
Protein	2 g	
Vitamin A		2%
Vitamin C		25%
Calcium		5%
Iron		2%

Carbohydrate Choice 1

EXCHANGES: 1 Vegetable, $^1/_2$ Fat, $^1/_2$ Fruit

PREPARATION

1. Place all the salad ingredients in a large mixing bowl.

2. In a small bowl, whisk together all the dressing ingredients until smooth.

3. Spoon the dressing over the salad, toss and serve.

✳ Salad may be stored in an airtight container in the refrigerator for up to 5 days.

CABBAGE & BABY RADISH SALAD

Radishes are rich in vitamin C, folic acid, and potassium. They are also a good source of vitamin B6, riboflavin, magnesium, copper and calcium.

INGREDIENTS

5 cups cabbage, thinly sliced
2 cups bean sprouts
10 baby radishes, thoroughly washed and julienned

For the dressing:
1 tablespoon olive oil
2 tablespoons low-sodium soy sauce

6 SERVINGS

SERVING SIZE: 1 cup, 120 g, 4 oz.

Calories per serving	50	% Daily Value
Calories from fat	20	
Total Fat	2 g	3%
Saturated Fat	1 g	4%
Cholesterol	0 mg	0%
Sodium	195 mg	8%
Total Carbohydrates	7 g	2%
Sugars	3 g	
Dietary Fiber	2 g	8%
Protein	4 g	
Vitamin A		6%
Vitamin C		77%
Calcium		4%
Iron		2%
Carbohydrate Choice	1/2	

EXCHANGES: 1 Vegetable, 1/2 Fat

PREPARATION

1. Place all the salad ingredients in a large mixing bowl.

2. In a small bowl, whisk together the olive oil and soy sauce until smooth.

3. Drizzle the dressing over the salad, toss and serve.

✳ Salad may be stored in an airtight container in the refrigerator for up to 3 days.

FRESH BEET SALAD

In this salad, the beets are uncooked, and therefore maintain the maximum amounts vitamins and minerals.

INGREDIENTS

3 cups (3 large beets) peeled and shredded
1 Granny Smith apple, peeled, cored and shredded
1 celery rib, thinly sliced
1 cup parsley, coarsely chopped
2 tablespoons walnuts

For the dressing:
$1/4$ cup fresh lemon juice
1 teaspoon honey

6 SERVINGS

SERVING SIZE: 1 cup, 120 g, about 4 oz.

| Calories per serving | 70 | % Daily |
Calories from fat	30	Value
Total Fat	3 g	4%
Saturated Fat	0 g	0%
Cholesterol	0 mg	0%
Sodium	85 mg	4%
Total Carbohydrates	12 g	4%
Sugars	8 g	
Dietary Fiber	3 g	13%
Protein	2 g	
Vitamin A		20%
Vitamin C		30%
Calcium		2%
Iron		8%

Carbohydrate Choice   1

EXCHANGES: 1 Vegetable, $1/2$ Fat, $1/2$ Fruit

PREPARATION

1. Place all the salad ingredients in a large mixing bowl.

2. In a small bowl, whisk together the lemon juice and honey until smooth.

3. Drizzle the dressing over the salad, toss, allow it to stand at room temperature for 10 minutes and then serve.

∗ Salad may be stored in an airtight container in the refrigerator for up to 3 days.

¤ *Fresh Beet Salad*

¤ *Tangy Chicken Salad*

TANGY CHICKEN SALAD

This is a salad that works great as a whole meal because it contains protein and vegetables, which contain all the daily recommended intake of vitamin A.

INGREDIENTS

1 tablespoon olive oil
$1/2$ pound skinless, boneless chicken breasts, cut into strips
4 hearts of romaine lettuce, coarsely chopped
2 carrots, peeled and shredded
1 red apple, cored and sliced
1 tablespoon unsweetened dried cranberries

For the dressing:
1 tablespoon olive oil
1 tablespoon honey
1 tablespoon low-sodium soy sauce
3 tablespoons fresh lemon juice
1 garlic clove, minced
1 small yellow onion, finely chopped
Freshly ground pepper

4 SERVINGS

SERVING SIZE: $1^1/2$ cups, 210 g, 7 oz

		% Daily
Calories per serving	160	% Daily
Calories from fat	50	Value
Total Fat	6 g	9%
Saturated Fat	1 g	4%
Cholesterol	30 mg	10%
Sodium	140 mg	6%
Total Carbohydrates	14 g	4%
Sugars	8 g	
Dietary Fiber	2 g	7%
Protein	12 g	
Vitamin A		112%
Vitamin C		16%
Calcium		5%
Iron		10%

Carbohydrate Choice   1

EXCHANGES: 1 Vegetable, $1^1/2$ Lean Meat, $1/2$ Fruit, 1 Fat

PREPARATION

1. Prepare the dressing: Stir together all ingredients for the dressing in a medium bowl. Allow to stand at room temperature for 10 minutes.

2. Heat the olive oil in a large skillet over medium heat and add the chicken strips. Sauté for 5-7 minutes, until the chicken is completely cooked through. Remove from heat, allow the chicken to stand at room temperature for 5 minutes, and then add it to the prepared dressing.

3. Place the lettuce, carrots, apple and cranberries in a large serving bowl.

4. Add the chicken mixture, toss and serve.

ENDIVE SALAD WITH HEARTS OF PALM & SHRIMP

Endive contains many vitamins and minerals, especially folate and vitamins A and K.

INGREDIENTS

1 whole endive, cleaned and leaves separated

1 tablespoon fresh lemon juice

2 cups hearts of palm, washed, drained and cut into $1/2$-inch slices

2 cups cherry tomatoes, halved

7 oz. shrimp, fresh or frozen, cooked, peeled, deveined and chilled

$1/2$ cup Cocktail Sauce (see page 75)

PREPARATION

1. Place the endive leaves on a large, shallow serving platter and drizzle with 1 tablespoon of lemon juice.

2. Evenly arrange the hearts of palm slices and cherry tomatoes on the endive leaves. Place the shrimp on top, drizzle Cocktail Sauce over shrimp and serve.

6 SERVINGS

SERVING SIZE: 1¼ cups, 200 g, 7 oz.

		% Daily Value
Calories per serving	80	
Calories from fat	30	
Total Fat	3 g	4%
Saturated Fat	0 g	0%
Cholesterol	40 mg	13%
Sodium	345 mg	14%
Total Carbohydrates	7 g	2%
Sugars	1 g	
Dietary Fiber	4 g	16%
Protein	8 g	
Vitamin A		37%
Vitamin C		30%
Calcium		7%
Iron		13%

Carbohydrate Choice $1/2$

EXCHANGES: 1$1/2$ Vegetable, $1/2$ Fat, $1/2$ Lean Meat

SMOKED SALMON, MANGO & TOFU SALAD

This recipe combines ingredients that surprisingly work great together to make a healthy and refreshing salad to eat for lunch or as a side for dinner.

INGREDIENTS

3 oz. light tofu, cubed
1 tablespoon low-sodium soy sauce
1 head romaine lettuce, coarsely chopped
1 ripe mango, cut into $1/4$-inch cubes
$1/2$ ripe avocado, thinly sliced
2 oz. smoked salmon, thinly sliced

For the dressing:
$1/2$ cup fresh lemon juice
1 teaspoon Dijon mustard
1 teaspoon honey

6 SERVINGS

SERVING SIZE: 1 cup, 150 g, 5 oz.		
Calories per serving	120	% Daily
Calories from fat	40	Value
Total Fat	5 g	8%
Saturated Fat	1 g	4%
Cholesterol	20 mg	7%
Sodium	120 mg	5%
Total Carbohydrates	11 g	4%
Sugars	9 g	
Dietary Fiber	3 g	12%
Protein	10 g	
Vitamin A		13%
Vitamin C		45%
Calcium		7%
Iron		9%
Carbohydrate Choice	1	

EXCHANGES: 1 Vegetable, $1/2$ Fruit, 1 Lean Meat, $1/2$ Fat

PREPARATION

1. Marinate the tofu and soy sauce together for 10 minutes.

2. Place the lettuce, mango, avocado and smoked salmon in a large serving bowl. Top with the tofu and soy sauce.

3. Mix all the ingredients for the dressing together and pour over the salad. Toss and allow to sit at room temperature for 10 minutes before serving.

MAIN
COURSES

BAKED SALMON IN PARCHMENT PAPER

Cooking fish in parchment paper actually steams the fish in the oven, preserving its juices and flavors, and preventing it from drying out. The parchment paper acts as an envelope, providing a festive way to not only prepare, but also serve the fish.

INGREDIENTS

$1/4$ cup fresh lemon juice
4 tablespoons Dijon mustard
$1/2$ cup fresh orange juice
2 teaspoons honey
1 tablespoon olive oil
Freshly ground pepper
2 pounds salmon fillet (pink or wild Atlantic)

For garnish:
$1/4$ cup parsley, chopped

10 SERVINGS

SERVING SIZE: 1 slice of fish + sauce, 120 g, about 4 oz.

Calories per serving	160	% Daily
Calories from fat	50	Value
Total Fat	6 g	9%
Saturated Fat	1 g	5%
Cholesterol	45 mg	15%
Sodium	100 mg	4%
Total Carbohydrates	5 g	2%
Sugars	0 g	
Dietary Fiber	1 g	0%
Protein	22 g	
Vitamin A		5%
Vitamin C		16%
Calcium		2%
Iron		1%
Carbohydrate Choice	0	

EXCHANGES: 1 Vegetable, 3 Lean Meat, $1/2$ Fat

PREPARATION

1. Preheat oven to 400ºF.

2. In a medium bowl, mix together the lemon juice, 2 tablespoons of the mustard, orange juice, honey, olive oil and freshly ground pepper.

3. Place the salmon onto a piece of parchment paper, skin side down, and brush with the remaining 2 tablespoons of mustard.

4. Pour the prepared marinade over the salmon and fold in the sides of the parchment paper, creating an envelope.

5. Bake for 16-18 minutes, until salmon flakes easily with a fork. Garnish with chopped parsley and serve.

BAKED SALMON WITH TOMATOES

Use fresh Atlantic or pink salmon, which arc both high in omega-3 fatty acids. This recipe also works well with delicate white fish, such as sea bass or tilapia.

4 SERVINGS

SERVING SIZE: 1 slice of fish + tomatoes, 210 g, 7 oz.		
Calories per serving	180	% Daily
Calories from fat	60	Value
Total Fat	7 g	11%
Saturated Fat	1 g	4%
Cholesterol	60 mg	20%
Sodium	490 mg	20%
Total Carbohydrates	5 g	2%
Sugars	3 g	
Dietary Fiber	1 g	0%
Protein	22 g	
Vitamin A		14%
Vitamin C		30%
Calcium		3%
Iron		10%
Carbohydrate Choice	**0**	

EXCHANGES: 1 Vegetable, 3 Lean Meat, $^1/_2$ Fat

INGREDIENTS

1 pound salmon fillet
1 yellow onion, thinly sliced
1 garlic clove, thinly sliced
3 tomatoes, thinly sliced
1 teaspoon salt
Freshly ground pepper

PREPARATION

1. Preheat oven to 450ºF.

2. Place the salmon in a large baking dish and cover with onions, garlic, tomatoes, salt and pepper.

3. Bake for 15-17 minutes, until salmon flakes easily with a fork and serve.

SPICY SHRIMP IN COCONUT MILK

Sometimes fish recipes can come off as boring; this one is anything but boring and is still considered quite healthy. Accompany this flavorful dish with freshly steamed rice.

4 SERVINGS

SERVING SIZE: about 2 cups, 210 g, 7 oz.

		% Daily Value
Calories per serving	170	
Calories from fat	60	
Total Fat	7 g	11%
Saturated Fat	5 g	26%
Cholesterol	145 mg	48%
Sodium	300 mg	13%
Total Carbohydrates	3 g	1%
Sugars	1 g	
Dietary Fiber	1 g	0%
Protein	19 g	
Vitamin A		19%
Vitamin C		30%
Calcium		7%
Iron		1%
Carbohydrate Choice	0	

EXCHANGES: 1 Vegetable, 2½ Lean Meat, ½ Fat

INGREDIENTS

2 teaspoons butter
15 oz. fresh shrimp, uncooked, peeled, with tails on and deveined
1½ cups light coconut milk
²/₃ cup Sweet Chili Sauce (see page 58)

PREPARATION

1. Heat the butter in a large skillet over medium heat and add the shrimp. Cook for 2-3 minutes, until shrimp is pink.

2. Add the coconut milk and Sweet Chili Sauce, cook for an additional 3-4 minutes and serve warm.

STEAMED SEA BASS ROLLS WITH SPINACH

Serve this dish with a side dish of brown rice for a complete and hearty meal. The spinach provides an excellent source of iron.

INGREDIENTS

$^1/_4$ cup fresh lemon juice

6 sea bass fillets (about 5 oz. per fillet)

4 cups fresh spinach leaves

1 teaspoon dried tarragon

1 yellow onion, finely chopped

2 carrots, peeled and cut into small cubes

2 celery ribs, thinly sliced

2 leeks, thinly sliced, white part only

2 garlic cloves, minced

$^1/_2$ cup dry white wine

2 cups water

$^1/_4$ cup parsley

1 tablespoon cornstarch, dissolved in $^1/_2$ cup of warm water

6 SERVINGS

SERVING SIZE: 1 fish fillet + 1 cup of cooked vegetables, 350 g, about 12 oz.

		% Daily Value
Calories per serving	220	
Calories from fat	30	
Total Fat	4 g	6%
Saturated Fat	1 g	4%
Cholesterol	115 mg	38%
Sodium	160 mg	6%
Total Carbohydrates	17 g	6%
Sugars	5 g	
Dietary Fiber	3 g	12%
Protein	28 g	
Vitamin A		126%
Vitamin C		25%
Calcium		8%
Iron		19%

Carbohydrate Choice   1

EXCHANGES: 3$^1/_2$ Vegetable, 3 Lean Meat

PREPARATION

1. Prepare the fish rolls: Pour the lemon juice over the sea bass fillets and evenly place spinach leaves on top of fillets. Sprinkle tarragon over fillets. Roll up fillets and secure with toothpicks. Set aside.

2. Place the onion, carrots, celery, leeks, garlic, wine, water and parsley in a large saucepan and cook on low heat for 10 minutes.

3. Place the fish rolls on top of the vegetables and cook for 6-8 minutes until fish flakes easily with a fork. Remove fish from saucepan, using a slotted spoon.

4. Increase heat to high and bring vegetables to a boil. Lower heat, add the dissolved cornstarch and stir until thickened.

5. Place vegetables into a serving dish and top with the cooked fish rolls.

BAKED MEDITERRANEAN HALIBUT

Halibut is low in saturated fat and sodium. It is a good source of vitamin B6, vitamin B12, magnesium and potassium, and very high in protein.

INGREDIENTS

4 halibut fillets, (about 5 oz. per fillet)
1/2 cup fresh lemon juice
1 teaspoon salt
1 tablespoon olive oil
2 yellow onions, finely chopped
2 red bell peppers, cut into thin strips
3 tomatoes, thinly sliced
3 garlic cloves, minced
1 cup parsley, chopped
1 cup cilantro, chopped
1 teaspoon cumin
Freshly ground black pepper
1 cayenne pepper (optional)
15 green olives, pitted
1 teaspoon dry tarragon

4 SERVINGS

SERVING SIZE: 1 piece of fish + 1 cup sauce, 400 g, 13 oz.

Calories per serving	270	% Daily
Calories from fat	60	Value
Total Fat	9 g	11%
Saturated Fat	1 g	6%
Cholesterol	105 mg	35%
Sodium	580 mg	24%
Total Carbohydrates	21 g	7%
Sugars	9 g	
Dietary Fiber	5 g	20%
Protein	33 g	
Vitamin A		93%
Vitamin C		70%
Calcium		12%
Iron		13%
Carbohydrate Choice	1 1/2	

EXCHANGES: 4 Vegetable, 3 1/2 Lean Meat 1/2 Fat

PREPARATION

1. Place fish fillets in a large bowl and marinade with the lemon juice and salt for 1 hour in the refrigerator.

2. Preheat oven to 400ºF.

3. Heat the olive oil in a pan over medium heat, add the onions and sauté for 5 minutes, until translucent.

4. Place the marinated fish in a large baking dish and pour over the cooked onions. Add the bell peppers, tomato slices and garlic to the baking dish.

5. In a bowl, mix together the parsley, cilantro, cumin, ground pepper, cayenne pepper, olives and tarragon. Pour mixture over the fish and vegetables.

6. Cover with aluminum foil and bake for 25-30 minutes, until fish flakes easily with a fork. Serve warm.

SPICY HALIBUT WITH VEGETABLES

In this recipe, the fish is complemented with a vegetable-rich sauce, providing iron and vitamin C.

INGREDIENTS

2 tablespoons olive oil

1 large yellow onion, finely chopped

3 garlic cloves, coarsely chopped

1/2 teaspoon ground caraway seeds

3 red bell peppers, cut into thin strips

1 spicy red chili pepper, thinly sliced

3 cups water

1 tablespoon cumin

1/2 teaspoon freshly ground black pepper

1 teaspoon cayenne pepper

1 tablespoon paprika

1 teaspoon coarse salt

6 halibut steaks (about 5 oz. per steak)

1/4 cup fresh lemon juice

1 teaspoon lemon zest

1/2 cup parsley, chopped

1/2 cup cilantro, chopped

6 SERVINGS

SERVING SIZE: 1 piece of fish + 1 cup sauce, 350 g, 12 oz.

		% Daily Value
Calories per serving	230	
Calories from fat	70	
Total Fat	8 g	12%
Saturated Fat	1 g	4%
Cholesterol	110 mg	37%
Sodium	460 mg	19%
Total Carbohydrates	8 g	3%
Sugars	4 g	
Dietary Fiber	2 g	8%
Protein	33 g	
Vitamin A		60%
Vitamin C		70%
Calcium		8%
Iron		7%
Carbohydrate Choice	1/2	

EXCHANGES: 1 1/2 Vegetable, 4 Lean Meat

PREPARATION

1. Heat the olive oil in a large, deep, heavy skillet over medium heat. Add the onions and garlic and cook for 5 minutes, until translucent.

2. Add the caraway seeds and cook for another minute.

3. Add the bell peppers and chili pepper, and continue to cook for an additional 10 minutes.

4. Increase heat to high, add water and bring to a boil. Lower heat and add the cumin, black pepper, cayenne pepper, paprika and salt. Mix well.

5. Place the fish fillets on top of the sauce, and pour lemon juice and lemon zest over the fillets. Sprinkle with the chopped parsley and cilantro and continue to cook over low heat for another 25 minutes, uncovered, until fish flakes easily with a fork. Serve warm.

SEA BASS WITH ZUCCHINI

This Thai-inspired dish is a really easy recipe to prepare and packed with flavor.

INGREDIENTS

1 tablespoon olive oil
4 shallots, finely chopped
2 small zucchini, chopped into small cubes
2 garlic cloves, minced
$^1/_4$ cup low-sodium soy sauce
$^1/_4$ cup dry white wine
1 teaspoon honey
$^1/_4$ cup Sweet Chili Sauce (see page 58)
4 sea bass fillets (about 5 oz. per fillet)

4 SERVINGS

SERVING SIZE: 1 fillet of fish + $^1/_2$ cup vegetables, 240 g, 8 oz.		
Calories per serving	190	% Daily
Calories from fat	50	Value
Total Fat	5 g	8%
Saturated Fat	1 g	4%
Cholesterol	100 mg	33%
Sodium	540 mg	23%
Total Carbohydrates	7 g	2%
Sugars	1 g	
Dietary Fiber	1 g	4%
Protein	26 g	
Vitamin A		2%
Vitamin C		25%
Calcium		4%
Iron		11%
Carbohydrate Choice	$^1/_2$	

EXCHANGES: 1$^1/_2$ Vegetable, 2$^1/_2$ Lean Meat, 1 Fat

PREPARATION

1. Preheat oven to 425ºF.

2. In a large skillet, heat olive oil, add the shallots and sauté for 5 minutes, until translucent. Add the zucchini and cook for another 2-3 minutes, until softened.

3. Add the garlic, soy sauce, wine, honey and Sweet Chili Sauce and cook for an additional 2 minutes and then remove from heat.

4. Place each fish fillet onto a large piece of aluminum foil, skin side down.

5. Evenly spoon the prepared mixture onto each fillet and fold in the sides of the aluminum foil, securing it closed.

6. Bake for 10-12 minutes, until fish flakes easily with a fork. Serve warm.

CALAMARI IN WINE

Squid is naturally low in fat and in calories, but contains relatively high amounts of cholesterol, and should therefore be eaten in moderation. However, squid also contains potassium, which helps balance out salt intake.

INGREDIENTS

2 tablespoons whole-wheat flour
4 cups squid (calamari) rings
1 tablespoon olive oil

For the sauce:
1 tablespoon butter
1 yellow onion, finely chopped
2 garlic cloves, minced
4 ripe tomatoes, finely chopped
2 tablespoons tomato paste
$1/2$ cup water
$1/2$ cup semi-dry red wine

2 tablespoons brandy
$1/4$ teaspoon grated nutmeg
$1/2$ teaspoon coarse salt
Freshly ground pepper

For garnish:
$1/4$ cup parsley, chopped

6 SERVINGS

SERVING SIZE: $1^1/2$ cups, 210 g, 7 oz.

Calories per serving	160	% Daily
Calories from fat	40	Value
Total Fat	4 g	6%
Saturated Fat	1 g	4%
Cholesterol	185 mg	62%
Sodium	200 mg	8%
Total Carbohydrates	11 g	4%
Sugars	3 g	
Dietary Fiber	2 g	8%
Protein	13 g	
Vitamin A		18%
Vitamin C		10%
Calcium		5%
Iron		7%
Carbohydrate Choice	1	

EXCHANGES: 2 Vegetable, $1/2$ Fat, 2 Lean Meat

PREPARATION

1. Place the whole-wheat flour on a plate and gently roll squid rings in the flour.

2. Heat the olive oil in a large skillet over high heat and sauté the squid for 2-3 minutes, until golden. Remove skillet from heat.

3. Prepare the sauce: In a large saucepan over medium heat, heat the butter, add the onion and garlic and sauté for about 5 minutes, until translucent.

4. Lower heat and add the tomatoes, tomato paste and water, and cook for an additional 5 minutes.

5. Add the wine, brandy, nutmeg, salt and pepper and mix well. Add the calamari and cook for an additional 20 minutes.

6. Garnish with parsley and serve warm.

CATFISH WITH GARBANZO BEANS

This recipe contains both protein and carbohydrates, making it a hearty meal on its own. The garbanzo beans are a great source of fiber and iron.

INGREDIENTS

2 cups cooked garbanzo beans, without salt
2 garlic cloves, minced
1 teaspoon coarse salt
2 teaspoons cumin
1 cup parsley, chopped
1 cup cilantro, chopped
2 cups crushed tomatoes
4 catfish fillets (about 5 oz. per fillet)
1/4 cup fresh lemon juice
2 teaspoons cayenne pepper
Freshly ground black pepper

4 SERVINGS

SERVING SIZE: 1 fillet + 1 cup sauce, 300 g, 10 oz.

		% Daily Value
Calories per serving	270	
Calories from fat	50	
Total Fat	6 g	9%
Saturated Fat	1 g	4%
Cholesterol	80 mg	27%
Sodium	540 mg	23%
Total Carbohydrates	23 g	8%
Sugars	5 g	
Dietary Fiber	8 g	32%
Protein	31 g	
Vitamin A		50%
Vitamin C		20%
Calcium		10%
Iron		21%

Carbohydrate Choice 1 1/2

EXCHANGES: 1 1/2 Starch, 4 Lean Meat

PREPARATION

1. In a large, deep, heavy skillet, heat the garbanzo beans, garlic, salt, cumin, parsley, cilantro and crushed tomatoes over medium heat for 10-15 minutes.

2. Add water if sauce is too thick. Remove 3 tablespoons of the sauce and set aside.

3. Add the fish fillets, skin side down, and spoon the 3 tablespoons of sauce onto the fillets. Pour the lemon juice over the fillets and season with cayenne pepper and black pepper.

4. Cover and cook for 10-12 minutes, until fish flakes easily with a fork. Serve warm.

¤ *Catfish with Garbanzo Beans*

SEARED TUNA WITH WASABI HORSERADISH

Tuna fish is a great source of unsaturated fatty acids and is high in vitamin D. Serve this dish with a side of blanched green asparagus for a complete meal.

INGREDIENTS

2 tuna steaks (about 6 oz. per steak)
3 tablespoons low-sodium soy sauce
2 tablespoons fresh lemon juice
4 sheets of seaweed (nori)
1 tablespoon olive oil
$1/2$ cup purchased horseradish sauce
1 tablespoon wasabi paste
1 tablespoon black sesame seeds

4 SERVINGS

SERVING SIZE: 4$1/2$ thin slices of fish, 135 g, 4$1/2$ oz

Calories per serving	160	% Daily
Calories from fat	40	Value
Total Fat	4 g	7%
Saturated Fat	1 g	4%
Cholesterol	35 mg	12%
Sodium	395 mg	16%
Total Carbohydrates	5 g	2%
Sugars	2 g	
Dietary Fiber	1 g	0%
Protein	23 g	
Vitamin A		1%
Vitamin C		50%
Calcium		1%
Iron		2%
Carbohydrate Choice	**0**	

EXCHANGES: 3 Lean Meat, 1 Vegetable, $1/2$ Fat

PREPARATION

1. Place tuna steaks, soy sauce and lemon juice in a large bowl and marinate for 30 minutes.

2. Wrap each tuna steak with 2 sheets of nori.

3. Heat the olive oil in a large nonstick skillet over low heat and sear on each side for 3 minutes. The tuna should be cooked from the outside and still raw on the inside. (See Note below)

4. In a small bowl, mix together the horseradish sauce and wasabi paste.

5. Carefully slice the tuna into $1/4$-inch slices. Place tuna slices on a serving plate. Serve the wasabi sauce with the tuna and garnish with black sesame seeds.

Note: Eating raw fish carries a risk of foodborne illness. To avoid this risk, cook fish thoroughly.

¤ *Seared Tuna with Wasabi Horseradish*

¤ *Baked Tilapia*

BAKED TILAPIA

Tilapia is a great source of protein, while being low in saturated fat, calories, carbohydrates and sodium. It is also a source of phosphorus, niacin, selenium, vitamin B12 and potassium.

INGREDIENTS

4 tilapia fillets (about 5 oz. per fillet)
2 tablespoons olive oil
$1/4$ cup fresh lemon juice
2 garlic cloves, minced
1 cup cherry tomatoes, halved
$1/2$ cup Kalamata olives, pitted and chopped
1 teaspoon salt
1 teaspoon dried oregano

4 SERVINGS

SERVING SIZE: 1 fillet + sauce, 200 g, about 7 oz.		
Calories per serving	190	% Daily
Calories from fat	60	Value
Total Fat	7 g	10%
Saturated Fat	1 g	4%
Cholesterol	70 mg	23%
Sodium	270 mg	11%
Total Carbohydrates	3 g	1%
Sugars	1 g	
Dietary Fiber	1 g	0%
Protein	30 g	
Vitamin A		5%
Vitamin C		10%
Calcium		2%
Iron		9%
Carbohydrate Choice	0	

EXCHANGES: $1/2$ Vegetable, $1/2$ Fat, 3 $1/2$ Lean Meat

PREPARATION

1. Preheat oven to 425°F.

2. Place each fish fillet onto a piece of parchment paper, skin side down, and brush fillets with 1 tablespoon of the olive oil. Pour 1 tablespoon of lemon juice over each fillet.

3. Heat the remaining 1 tablespoon olive oil in a skillet over medium heat, add the garlic and sauté for 1 minute. Add the tomatoes, olives, salt and oregano, and cook for an additional 5 minutes. Remove from heat.

4. Evenly spoon the prepared tomato mixture onto each fillet and fold in the sides of the parchment paper, creating an envelope.

5. Bake for 10-12 minutes, until fish flakes easily with a fork. Serve warm.

CURRY CHICKEN WITH TOMATOES

The spices in this Indian-style dish, along with the rich tomato sauce, create a festive dish with chicken breasts.

INGREDIENTS

1 pound boneless, skinless chicken breasts, cut into 1 inch cubes
1 tablespoon canola oil
2 garlic cloves, minced
1 teaspoon ginger, finely grated
3 tomatoes, finely chopped
1 teaspoon coarse salt
$1/2$ teaspoon cumin
1 teaspoon curry powder
$1/2$ teaspoon cinnamon
$1/4$ cup water

For garnish:
1 cup cilantro leaves

4 SERVINGS

SERVING SIZE: about $3/4$ cup, 180 g, 6 oz.

Calories per serving	150	% Daily
Calories from fat	40	Value
Total Fat	4 g	6%
Saturated Fat	1 g	4%
Cholesterol	60 mg	20%
Sodium	425 mg	18%
Total Carbohydrates	4 g	1%
Sugars	2 g	
Dietary Fiber	1 g	0%
Protein	24 g	
Vitamin A		18%
Vitamin C		10%
Calcium		3%
Iron		3%
Carbohydrate Choice	**0**	

EXCHANGES: 1 Vegetable, 3 Lean Meat

PREPARATION

1. Spray a large nonstick skillet with oil spray and heat on high heat. Cook chicken cubes for about 5 minutes, until cooked through. Remove chicken from skillet.

2. Heat oil on medium heat, add the garlic and ginger and sauté for 2 minutes. Add the tomatoes, salt, cumin, curry powder and cinnamon, and cook for another 5 minutes.

3. Add the chicken and water, and cook for an additional 5 minutes. Garnish with cilantro leaves and serve warm.

✳ Entrée may be stored in an airtight container in the refrigerator for up to 4 days.

¤ *Curry Chicken with Tomatoes*

COQ AU VIN (CHICKEN IN RED WINE)

This French-inspired dish is lower in calories than the original version. Serve it with a side of brown rice to soak up the delicious sauce.

INGREDIENTS

3 pounds chicken, skinless and cut into pieces

2 tablespoons whole-wheat flour

1 tablespoon butter

1 cup water

$^1/_2$ cup dry red wine

3 garlic cloves, thinly sliced

3 bay leaves

8 allspice berries

3 sprigs fresh thyme

4 oz. low-fat smoked sausage, thinly sliced

4 cups white mushrooms

2 yellow onions, thinly sliced

2 carrots, peeled and thinly sliced

3 sprigs parsley

8 SERVINGS

SERVING SIZE: about 1$^1/_4$ cups, 280 g, 9 oz.

		% Daily Value
Calories per serving	250	
Calories from fat	80	
Total Fat	9 g	14%
Saturated Fat	2 g	8%
Cholesterol	110 mg	37%
Sodium	485 mg	20%
Total Carbohydrates	9 g	3%
Sugars	3 g	
Dietary Fiber	2 g	8%
Protein	29 g	
Vitamin A		72%
Vitamin C		10%
Calcium		5%
Iron		11%

Carbohydrate Choice $^1/_2$

EXCHANGES: 2 Vegetable, 4$^1/_2$ Lean Meat

PREPARATION

1. Dredge the chicken pieces in the flour, shaking off any remaining flour.

2. Heat the butter in a large nonstick skillet over high heat and cook the chicken, until browned on all sides.

3. Reduce heat. Add water, wine, garlic, bay leaves, allspice and thyme. Cook over medium heat for 7 minutes.

4. Add the sausage, mushrooms, onions, carrots and parsley to the skillet. Cover and simmer for 35 minutes, until chicken is completely cooked through and vegetables are tender. Serve warm.

✳ Entrée may be stored in an airtight container in the refrigerator for up to 4 days.

LEMON CHICKEN SCALLOPINI

This Italian-inspired dish is a great way to serve chicken.

INGREDIENTS

2 tablespoons whole-wheat flour
$^1/_2$ teaspoon salt
Freshly ground pepper
1 pound chicken breast cutlets, pounded very thin
2 tablespoons canola oil
$^1/_4$ cup fresh lemon juice
$^1/_3$ cup water
1 tablespoon lemon zest

4 SERVINGS

SERVING SIZE: 1 chicken cutlet + sauce, about 165 g, 5$^1/_2$ oz.

		% Daily Value
Calories per serving	210	
Calories from fat	50	
Total Fat	5 g	8%
Saturated Fat	1 g	4%
Cholesterol	120 mg	40%
Sodium	165 mg	7%
Total Carbohydrates	4 g	5%
Sugars	0 g	
Dietary Fiber	1 g	13%
Protein	34 g	
Vitamin A		1%
Vitamin C		15%
Calcium		6%
Iron		0%
Carbohydrate Choice	**0**	

EXCHANGES: $^1/_2$ Fat, 4 Lean Meat, 1 Vegetable

PREPARATION

1. Place the whole-wheat flour, salt and pepper onto a plate and mix. Lightly dredge the chicken cutlets in the flour, shaking off any remaining flour.

2. In a large nonstick skillet, heat the oil over high heat, and add the chicken cutlets. Cook for 2-3 minutes on each side, until golden. Remove only cutlets from skillet, leaving the oil.

3. Add the lemon juice, water and lemon zest to the skillet and continue to cook on high heat for 1-2 minutes, until the sauce becomes thick.

4. Pour sauce over chicken and serve warm.

✱ Entrée may be stored in an airtight container in the refrigerator for up to 4 days.

DRUMSTICKS WITH ORANGE JUICE & FENNEL

The fennel in this recipes cooks in both the juices of the orange and the chicken, making it soft and somewhat sweet with a mild anise taste.

6 SERVINGS

SERVING SIZE: 2 chicken drumsticks + 1/2 fennel and sauce, 240 g, 8 oz.

Calories per serving	200	% Daily
Calories from fat	40	Value
Total Fat	4 g	6%
Saturated Fat	1 g	4%
Cholesterol	75 mg	25%
Sodium	435 mg	18%
Total Carbohydrates	14 g	5%
Sugars	5 g	
Dietary Fiber	3 g	13%
Protein	23 g	
Vitamin A		4%
Vitamin C		15%
Calcium		6%
Iron		12%

Carbohydrate Choice   1

EXCHANGES: 1 1/2 Vegetable, 3 Lean Meat, 1/2 Fruit

INGREDIENTS

1 garlic clove, minced
1/2 cup fresh orange juice
1 tablespoon honey
1 tablespoon + 1/2 cup water
1 teaspoon coarse salt
1 teaspoon fresh thyme leaves
12 skinless chicken drumsticks
1 yellow onion, thinly sliced
2 large fennel bulbs, trimmed and quartered
6 prunes, halved
1 cup orange, thinly sliced

PREPARATION

1. Preheat oven to 350ºF.

2. In a large bowl, mix together the garlic, orange juice, honey, 1 tablespoon of water, salt and thyme. Add the chicken to the bowl and allow it to marinate at room temperature for 15 minutes.

3. Place the onion and fennel into a large baking dish and place the chicken, including the marinade, on top. Pour in the remaining 1/2 cup water and evenly scatter the prunes and orange slices.

4. Cover with aluminum foil and bake for 40 minutes. Remove the aluminum foil and continue baking, uncovered, for an additional 15 minutes. Serve warm.

✳ Entrée may be stored in an airtight container in the refrigerator for up to 4 days.

¤ *Drumsticks with Orange Juice & Fennel*

CHICKEN CACCIATORE

This hearty recipe is full of nutritious ingredients. The tomatoes are high in lycopene, the chicken is a great source of protein, and the mushrooms are rich in dietary fiber.

INGREDIENTS

1 tablespoon canola oil

6 skinless chicken legs

7 cups white mushrooms, thinly sliced

3 cups portobello mushrooms, thinly sliced

2 cups crushed tomatoes

$1/2$ tablespoon lemon zest

$1/2$ teaspoon salt

Freshly ground pepper

6 SERVINGS

SERVING SIZE: 1 piece chicken + about 1 cup sauce, 350 g, 12 oz.

		% Daily Value
Calories per serving	290	
Calories from fat	90	
Total Fat	10 g	16%
Saturated Fat	2 g	8%
Cholesterol	185 mg	62%
Sodium	355 mg	15%
Total Carbohydrates	5 g	2%
Sugars	3 g	
Dietary Fiber	3 g	12%
Protein	42 g	
Vitamin A		7%
Vitamin C		11%
Calcium		3%
Iron		15%

Carbohydrate Choice   0

EXCHANGES: 1 Vegetable, 5$1/2$ Lean Meat

PREPARATION

1. Heat the oil in a large nonstick skillet and add the chicken. Cook until chicken is browned on each side.

2. Add the mushrooms and continue to cook for 5 minutes. Add the tomatoes, lemon zest, salt and pepper.

3. Cover and cook on low heat for 45 minutes. Serve warm.

✖ Entrée may be stored in an airtight container in the refrigerator for up to 4 days.

TURKEY CURRY

This is a great dish to make when entertaining because it's colorful, tasty and healthy all at the same time. Serve this dish with Indian Rice for a complete meal.

10 SERVINGS

SERVING SIZE: 1¹/₂ cups, 240 g, 8 oz.

		% Daily
Calories per serving	180	Value
Calories from fat	50	
Total Fat	6 g	9%
Saturated Fat	1 g	4%
Cholesterol	65 mg	22%
Sodium	485 mg	20%
Total Carbohydrates	11 g	4%
Sugars	2 g	
Dietary Fiber	1 g	4%
Protein	20 g	
Vitamin A		0%
Vitamin C		0%
Calcium		4%
Iron		11%

Carbohydrate Choice 1

EXCHANGES: ¹/₂ **Vegetable,** ¹/₂ **Starch,** 2¹/₂ **Lean Meat**

INGREDIENTS

2 tablespoons canola oil

2 pounds skinless, boneless dark meat turkey, cut into 1-inch cubes

3 yellow onions, chopped

1 garlic clove, minced

2 teaspoons coarse salt

2 Granny Smith apples, peeled and chopped

2 tablespoons whole-wheat flour

¹/₄ cup fresh lemon juice

3 cups water

2 tablespoons garam masala

¹/₂ teaspoon ground allspice

¹/₂ teaspoon freshly ground black pepper

¹/₂ teaspoon ground ginger

1 dried cayenne pepper (optional)

PREPARATION

1. Heat 1 tablespoon of the oil in a large nonstick skillet over medium heat and sauté the turkey for about 7 minutes, until browned. Remove the turkey from the skillet and set aside for later use.

2. Heat the remaining 1 tablespoon oil in the skillet over medium heat and add the onions. Sauté for 7-10 minutes, until golden. Add the garlic and 1 teaspoon of the salt, and cook for another minute.

3. Add the apples and continue cooking on medium heat for another 2-3 minutes. Add all the remaining ingredients including the remaining 1 teaspoon salt and cook for an additional 15 minutes, using a wooden spoon to stir frequently. Remove from heat.

4. Place apple mixture in a food processor and blend until smooth. Place sauce and turkey back into the skillet. Cover and cook for an additional 30 minutes on low heat. Serve with Indian Rice (see page 152).

✳ Entrée may be stored in an airtight container in the refrigerator for up to 5 days.

CHICKEN WITH LENTILS & TOMATOES

The nutritional value of this dish seems relatively high, but that's because the carbohydrate is cooked along with the protein in this dish, making it a complete meal. The lentils in this dish are a good source of dietary fiber.

INGREDIENTS

1 tablespoon canola oil
1 yellow onion, finely chopped
3 garlic cloves, thinly sliced
6 skinless chicken legs
6 ripe tomatoes, peeled and coarsely chopped
1 teaspoon coarse salt
1 teaspoon cumin
$1/2$ teaspoon cinnamon
Freshly ground pepper
1 cup brown lentils, rinsed and drained
$2 1/2$ cups water
1 tablespoon fresh rosemary leaves

6 SERVINGS

SERVING SIZE: 1 piece chicken, 380 g, about 13 oz.

Calories per serving	390	% Daily Value
Calories from fat	90	
Total Fat	10 g	16%
Saturated Fat	2 g	11%
Cholesterol	150 mg	50%
Sodium	460 mg	19%
Total Carbohydrates	22 g	7%
Sugars	3 g	
Dietary Fiber	10 g	40%
Protein	39 g	
Vitamin A		19%
Vitamin C		10%
Calcium		3%
Iron		11%

Carbohydrate Choice 1$1/2$

EXCHANGES: 1$1/2$ Vegetable, 6 Lean Meat, 1 Starch

PREPARATION

1. In a large, heavy-bottomed saucepan, heat the oil over medium heat and add the onions. Sauté for 8-10 minutes, until golden. Add the garlic and sauté for another 2 minutes.

2. Add the chicken and cook on all sides until browned. Remove chicken from saucepan.

3. Add the tomatoes, salt, cumin, cinnamon, and pepper and cook for about 15 minutes, until the tomatoes have softened.

4. Return the chicken to the saucepan, add the lentils, water and rosemary and cook for 45 minutes, until the lentils and chicken are completely cooked. Add more water during cooking if needed. Serve warm.

✱ Entrée may be stored in an airtight container in the refrigerator for up to 4 days.

¤ *Chicken with Lentils & Tomatoes*

ROASTED SIRLOIN WITH TOMATOES

Tomatoes actually gain nutritional value when cooked. Lycopene, the most vital nutrient found in tomatoes, has been found to be a potential agent for prevention of some types of cancers, particularly prostate cancer. The lycopene is concentrated when cooked.

10 SERVINGS

SERVING SIZE: 2 slices sirloin + 1 baked tomato, 240 g, 8 oz.

		% Daily Value
Calories per serving	200	
Calories from fat	60	
Total Fat	7 g	10%
Saturated Fat	3 g	14%
Cholesterol	90 mg	30%
Sodium	385 mg	16%
Total Carbohydrates	6 g	2%
Sugars	4 g	
Dietary Fiber	1 g	4%
Protein	29 g	
Vitamin A		16%
Vitamin C		10%
Calcium		3%
Iron		29%

Carbohydrate Choice ¹/₂

EXCHANGES: 1 Vegetable, 4 Lean Meat

INGREDIENTS

3 pounds sirloin, fat trimmed
6 tablespoons red wine vinegar
1 teaspoon fresh rosemary leaves
1 teaspoon salt
Freshly ground pepper
1 large yellow onion, sliced into ¹/₄-inch slices
8 tomatoes, cut with a shallow cross on the bottom + 2 tomatoes, sliced

PREPARATION

1. Place the sirloin in a large bowl. In a separate small bowl, mix together the vinegar, rosemary, salt and pepper. Rub the mixture onto the sirloin, cover with plastic wrap and refrigerate overnight.

2. Remove sirloin from refrigerator and preheat oven to 425°F.

3. Place ¹/₂ of the onion slices onto the bottom of a roasting pan. Place the sirloin on top, and cover with the remaining onion and sliced tomatoes. Place the whole tomatoes around the sirloin.

4. Cover roasting pan with aluminum foil and roast for 40-45 minutes. Remove foil and continue to roast for an additional 10 minutes.

5. Remove from oven and allow the roast to rest for 15 minutes.

6. Using a sharp knife, slice the roast into thin slices and serve with the baked tomatoes and the sauce from the roasting pan.

✱ Entrée may be stored in an airtight container in the refrigerator for up to 5 days.

ROAST BEEF WITH ROOT VEGETABLES

This recipe contains a variety of root vegetables which are rich in nutrients, such as vitamin A.

8 SERVINGS

SERVING SIZE: 1 slice of beef + 1 cup vegetables and sauce, 300 g, 10 oz.

		% Daily
Calories per serving	240	Value
Calories from fat	60	
Total Fat	7 g	11%
Saturated Fat	2 g	8%
Cholesterol	65 mg	22%
Sodium	380 mg	16%
Total Carbohydrates	17 g	6%
Sugars	6 g	
Dietary Fiber	3 g	12%
Protein	25 g	
Vitamin A		80%
Vitamin C		14%
Calcium		9%
Iron		16%

Carbohydrate Choice   1

EXCHANGES: 1 1/2 Vegetable, 1/2 Fat, 3 1/2 Lean Meat, 1/2 Starch

INGREDIENTS

2 pounds sirloin, fat trimmed
3 garlic cloves, sliced

For the seasoning:
1 teaspoon Dijon mustard
1 teaspoon honey
1/2 teaspoon coarse salt
1/2 teaspoon freshly ground pepper

For the sauce:
2 tablespoons all-purpose flour
2 tablespoons canola oil
3 cups yellow onions, coarsely chopped
1 cup carrots, peeled and coarsely chopped
1 cup celeriac, peeled and coarsely chopped
2 cups celery ribs, coarsely chopped
5 pitted prunes
1/2 cup dry red wine
3 cups water
1/2 teaspoon salt
Freshly ground pepper

PREPARATION

1. Using a knife, make small slits in the sirloin and place the garlic slices inside the slits. In a large bowl, mix together all the ingredients for the seasoning. Rub the seasoning into the meat. Cover and refrigerate overnight.

2. Remove from refrigerator 30 minutes before cooking. Lightly dredge the sirloin in flour.

3. Heat 1 tablespoon of the oil in a large skillet over high heat and sear the sirloin, until browned on each side.

4. In a Dutch oven, heat the remaining 1 tablespoon oil over medium heat and add onions. Sauté for about 7 minutes, until golden. Add the carrots, celeriac, celery, prunes, wine and water, and bring to a boil over high heat.

5. Reduce heat, add the salt, pepper and sirloin and continue to cook, covered, for 1 hour. Uncover and cook for another 30 minutes over low heat. Serve warm.

✱ Entrée may be stored in an airtight container in the refrigerator for up to 5 days.

ZUCCHINI MEATBALLS IN TOMATO & PEA SAUCE

The addition of zucchini to these meatballs preserves their moistness, whereas regular meatballs have the tendency to dry out when cooked or reheated. Serve with a side of brown or white basmati rice for a complete meal.

INGREDIENTS

For the meatballs:
1/2 pound extra-lean ground beef
2 zucchini, finely grated and drained
1 yellow onion, finely chopped
1 garlic clove, minced
1 egg, beaten
3/4 cup old-fashioned oats
1 cup parsley
1 teaspoon salt
1/2 teaspoon turmeric
2 teaspoons paprika
1 teaspoon cumin

For the sauce:
1 tablespoon olive oil
1 yellow onion, finely chopped
2 garlic cloves, minced
1 red bell pepper, cut into 1/2-inch cubes
3 tomatoes, peeled and coarsely chopped
2 celery ribs, thinly sliced
3 tablespoons tomato paste
3 cups water
2 teaspoons salt
1/2 teaspoon turmeric
1 teaspoon paprika
1 teaspoon cumin
2 cups frozen green peas
1/4 cup fresh lemon juice

6 SERVINGS

SERVING SIZE: 3 meatballs + 1 1/2 cups sauce, about 420 g, 16 oz.

		% Daily Value
Calories per serving	240	
Calories from fat	60	
Total Fat	7 g	11%
Saturated Fat	2 g	12%
Cholesterol	80 mg	23%
Sodium	670 mg	28%
Total Carbohydrates	29 g	10%
Sugars	9 g	
Dietary Fiber	6 g	25%
Protein	17 g	
Vitamin A		52%
Vitamin C		70%
Calcium		6%
Iron		19%

Carbohydrate Choice 2

EXCHANGES: 4 Vegetable, 1 1/2 Lean Meat, 1/2 Fat, 1/2 Starch

PREPARATION

1. Place all the ingredients for the meatballs in a food processor fitted with a metal blade and process until all ingredients are combined. Set aside, at room temperature, for later use.

2. Meanwhile, prepare the sauce: Heat the olive oil in a large saucepan over medium heat, add the onion and sauté for about 5-7 minutes, until translucent. Add the garlic and bell pepper and continue to sauté for 2-3 minutes. Add the tomatoes and celery and cook for an additional 10 minutes.

3. Increase heat, add the tomato paste, water, salt, turmeric, paprika and cumin, and bring to a boil. Reduce heat and simmer for an additional 45 minutes.

4. Meanwhile, roll the meatballs: With slightly wet hands, form 18 meatballs.

For garnish:

1 cup parsley, finely chopped

5. Add the meatballs to the sauce and add the peas and lemon juice. Cook for 15-20 minutes, until the meat is completely cooked through. Garnish with chopped parsley and serve.

✻ Entrée may be stored in an airtight container in the refrigerator for up to 5 days.

STUFFED ZUCCHINI

Zucchini is low in calories and is a good source of folate, potassium and vitamin A.

5 SERVINGS

SERVING SIZE: 1 zucchini + 1/2 cup sauce, about 480 g, 16 oz.

		% Daily Value
Calories per serving	240	
Calories from fat	90	
Total Fat	10 g	16%
Saturated Fat	4 g	16%
Cholesterol	55 mg	18%
Sodium	605 mg	25%
Total Carbohydrates	13 g	4%
Sugars	9 g	
Dietary Fiber	4 g	17%
Protein	22 g	
Vitamin A		39%
Vitamin C		70%
Calcium		8%
Iron		21%

Carbohydrate Choice   1

EXCHANGES: 2 1/2 Vegetable, 3 Lean Meat, 1/2 Fat

INGREDIENTS

5 large zucchini
1 large yellow onion, finely chopped
1 cup parsley, finely chopped
1 pound extra-lean ground beef
1 teaspoon salt
1 teaspoon paprika
Freshly ground pepper

For the sauce:
4 ripe tomatoes, peeled and finely chopped
3 tablespoons tomato paste
1 cup water
1 teaspoon salt
1 teaspoon paprika
Freshly ground pepper

PREPARATION

1. Cut the zucchini in half lengthwise and use a spoon to scoop out the flesh into a bowl. Set all aside for later use.

2. Preheat oven to 425ºF.

3. Place onion, zucchini flesh and parsley in a food processor fitted with a metal blade and process until smooth. Add beef, salt, paprika and pepper and process, until all ingredients are combined.

4. With wet hands, place the meat mixture equally into all of the zucchini halves; mixture should be piled up over the top. Place the filled zucchini halves into a large baking dish.

5. In a medium bowl, mix together all the ingredients for the sauce and pour over the stuffed zucchini.

6. Bake, uncovered, for 45-50 minutes, until zucchini are soft and the meat is cooked through.

✳ Entrée may be stored in an airtight container in the refrigerator for up to 5 days.

STUFFED ARTICHOKE HEARTS

This is an age-old recipe that was passed down to me from my mother-in-law. This recipe is a bit more difficult to prepare than the rest, but it is well worth the effort.

10 SERVINGS

SERVING SIZE: 1 stuffed artichoke + sauce, 180 g, 6 oz.

		% Daily
Calories per serving	170	Value
Calories from fat	80	
Total Fat	9 g	15%
Saturated Fat	2 g	8%
Cholesterol	45 mg	15%
Sodium	235 mg	10%
Total Carbohydrates	12 g	4%
Sugars	1 g	
Dietary Fiber	3 g	12%
Protein	10 g	
Vitamin A		2%
Vitamin C		10%
Calcium		3%
Iron		6%

Carbohydrate Choice   1

EXCHANGES: 1 Vegetable, 1 Lean Meat, 1¹/₂ Fat, ¹/₂ Starch

INGREDIENTS

Two 9-oz. packages frozen artichoke
  hearts, thawed

For the filling:
1 tablespoon olive oil
2 yellow onions, finely chopped
¹/₂ pound extra-lean ground beef
1 teaspoon coarse salt
Freshly ground pepper
2 tablespoons pine nuts

For the batter:
5 tablespoons whole-wheat flour
1 egg, beaten
³/₄ cup water

For the sauce:
3 tablespoons olive oil
¹/₂ cup water
1¹/₂ cups strained Chicken Broth
  (see page 25)
¹/₃ cup fresh lemon juice

PREPARATION

1. Prepare the filling: Heat the olive oil in a nonstick skillet over medium heat, add the onions and sauté for 5 minutes, until translucent.

2. Add the ground beef and cook for about 10 minutes, until browned. Add the salt, pepper and pine nuts and remove from heat. Allow to cool for 10 minutes.

3. Prepare the batter: In a medium bowl, mix together the flour, egg and water until batter is smooth.

4. With slightly wet hands, press the meat filling into the artichoke hearts. The filling should be piled up over the top.

5. Heat 3 tablespoons of olive oil in a large nonstick skillet over high heat.

6. Working quickly, using a slotted spoon, dip each stuffed artichoke heart into the batter and place, with the filling side down, into the skillet. Cook for 5 minutes and then turn them over to cook on the other side.

7. Pour the water, chicken broth and lemon juice into the skillet, lower heat and continue to cook, covered, for 30 minutes, until the artichokes are softened and the meat is cooked through. Serve warm.

✳ Entrée may be stored in an airtight container in the refrigerator for up to 4 days.

BAKED KABOBS

The spinach, in combination with the ground meat, leads to a very moist and flavorful dish, full of iron and rich in dietary fiber.

INGREDIENTS

3 cups fresh spinach leaves, steamed and drained of all liquid

2 cups yellow onion, finely chopped

2 garlic cloves, minced

1 cup parsley leaves, finely chopped

1 teaspoon cumin

1 teaspoon salt

Freshly ground pepper

1 pound extra-lean ground beef

6 SERVINGS

SERVING SIZE: 2 kabobs, 120 g, 4 oz.

		% Daily Value
Calories per serving	120	
Calories from fat	40	
Total Fat	4 g	6%
Saturated Fat	2 g	8%
Cholesterol	50 mg	17%
Sodium	325 mg	14%
Total Carbohydrates	4 g	1%
Sugars	1 g	
Dietary Fiber	1 g	4%
Protein	17 g	
Vitamin A		52%
Vitamin C		10%
Calcium		5%
Iron		22%
Carbohydrate Choice	0	

EXCHANGES: 1 Vegetable, 2 Lean Meat

PREPARATION

1. Preheat oven to 425ºF. Place all ingredients, excluding the beef, in a food processor fitted with a metal blade and process until smooth. Add the beef and continue to process until all ingredients are combined.

2. Using slightly wet hands, take a handful of meat (about 2 oz.) and create 12 elongated kabobs with your hands.

3. Cut out twelve 4-inch by 4-inch squares of parchment paper and wrap each kabob, twisting the edges like a candy wrapper.

4. Place kabobs in a baking pan and bake for 7 minutes. Serve warm.

✳ Entrée may be stored in an airtight container in the refrigerator for up to 5 days.

¤ *Baked Kabobs*

VEAL SCALLOPINI

It is very important to buy good quality, lean meat when preparing this dish, as the meat is the star in this recipe. Serve the veal next to cooked vegetables, salad or baked sweet potatoes for a complete meal.

INGREDIENTS

1 pound veal cutlets, pounded very thin
2 tablespoons whole-wheat flour
1 tablespoon butter
$1/2$ cup dry red wine
2 tablespoons water
Freshly ground pepper

4 SERVINGS

SERVING SIZE: 1 cutlet + sauce, about 150 g, 5 oz.

| Calories per serving | 180 | % Daily |
Calories from fat	50	Value
Total Fat	5 g	8%
Saturated Fat	2 g	8%
Cholesterol	100 mg	33%
Sodium	90 mg	4%
Total Carbohydrates	4 g	1%
Sugars	0 g	
Dietary Fiber	1 g	0%
Protein	24 g	
Vitamin A		0%
Vitamin C		0%
Calcium		2%
Iron		9%

Carbohydrate Choice 0

EXCHANGES: $1/2$ **Fat, 3 Lean Meat, 1 Vegetable**

PREPARATION

1. Lightly dredge the veal cutlets in the flour, shaking off any remaining flour.

2. In a large nonstick skillet, heat the butter over high heat, and add the veal cutlets. Cook for 2-3 minutes on each side, until golden and cooked through. Remove only cutlets from skillet and keep warm.

3. Add the red wine, water and pepper to the skillet and continue to cook on high heat for 2-3 minutes, until the sauce thickens slightly.

4. Pour sauce over veal and serve warm.

✻ Entrée may be stored in an airtight container in the refrigerator for up to 5 days.

MEAT & EGGPLANT PIE

Eggplants are not only low in calories, but also a rich source of dietary fiber, vitamins and minerals. Other essential minerals found in eggplants include potassium, manganese, magnesium and copper. Traditionally, eggplants are fried and therefore absorb a lot of oil. In this dish, only a small amount of oil is used.

8 SERVINGS

SERVING SIZE: 1 slice, 320g, 11 oz.

Calories per serving	210	% Daily
Calories from fat	60	Value
Total Fat	7 g	11%
Saturated Fat	2 g	8%
Cholesterol	55 mg	18%
Sodium	525 mg	22%
Total Carbohydrates	16 g	5%
Sugars	7 g	
Dietary Fiber	5 g	20%
Protein	20 g	
Vitamin A		58%
Vitamin C		10%
Calcium		5%
Iron		24%
Carbohydrate Choice	1	

EXCHANGES: 3 Vegetable, 1/2 Fat, 2 1/2 Lean Meat

INGREDIENTS

For the eggplants:
2 large eggplants, peeled and sliced lengthwise into 1/4-inch slices
1 teaspoon salt
Freshly ground pepper

For the pie:
2 tablespoons olive oil
1 yellow onion, finely chopped
1 1/2 pounds extra-lean ground beef
3 tomatoes, peeled and coarsely chopped
2 tablespoons tomato paste
1/2 cup dry red wine
1 teaspoon coarse salt
1 teaspoon freshly ground pepper
1/2 teaspoon cumin
1/2 teaspoon cinnamon
2 sprigs fresh thyme
1 carrot, peeled and coarsely chopped
2 leeks, white part only, sliced

PREPARATION

1. Preheat oven to 425ºF. Place eggplant slices on baking sheet lined with parchment paper and season with salt and pepper. Bake for 15 minutes, until softened, remove from oven and set aside for later use. Reduce temperature to 400ºF.

2. In a large nonstick skillet, heat 2 tablespoons of the olive oil on medium heat and sauté the onion for 7 minutes, until golden. Add the ground meat and cook for about 5-7 minutes, until browned.

3. Add the tomatoes, tomato paste, red wine, salt, pepper, cumin, cinnamon and thyme and cook, stirring frequently until the mixture thickens, for about 10 minutes. Remove from heat.

4. Line a round, deep, 9-inch baking dish with half of the baked eggplant, both on the bottom and sides. Add half of the meat mixture and then evenly place the carrots and leeks over the meat. Add the remaining meat mixture and then layer with the remaining baked eggplant. Cover with aluminum foil.

5. Bake for 45 minutes. Remove the aluminum foil and bake for an additional 15 minutes. Allow to cool at room temperature for 30 minutes.

6. Turn pie upside down onto a large serving plate and serve warm.

✴ May be stored in an airtight container in the refrigerator for up to 3 days.

VEGETABLES, RICE & PASTA

RICE NOODLE STIR-FRY WITH BROCCOLI & TOFU

Rice noodles, a staple in the Thai kitchen, can be found in the international section of any large supermarket.

4 SERVINGS

SERVING SIZE: 2 cups, 330 g, 10 oz.

		% Daily Value
Calories per serving	210	
Calories from fat	40	
Total Fat	4 g	7%
Saturated Fat	0 g	0%
Cholesterol	0 mg	0%
Sodium	270 mg	11%
Total Carbohydrates	31 g	10%
Sugars	4 g	
Dietary Fiber	6 g	24%
Protein	12 g	
Vitamin A		156%
Vitamin C		100%
Calcium		11%
Iron		12%

Carbohydrate Choice   2

EXCHANGES: 1½ Vegetable, 1½ Starch, 1 Lean Meat

INGREDIENTS

For the noodles:
3 oz. rice noodles
4 cups water, boiling

For the stir-fry:
1 tablespoon olive oil
2 garlic cloves, minced
8 oz. tofu, cut into 1-inch cubes
½ teaspoon sesame oil
1 large carrot, peeled and julienned
1 teaspoon grated fresh ginger
¼ teaspoon red pepper flakes (optional)
6 cups white mushrooms, thinly sliced
4 cups broccoli florets
1 teaspoon lemon zest
2 tablespoons low-sodium soy sauce

PREPARATION

1. Soak the rice noodles in large bowl with boiling water and allow noodles to stand for 5 minutes. Drain and set aside for later use.

2. Heat the olive oil in a large wok over medium heat, add the garlic and sauté for 2 minutes. Add the tofu and sesame oil and continue to cook for an additional 2 minutes.

3. Add the carrots, ginger and red pepper flakes, cook for another minute, and then add the mushrooms and cook for 2-3 minutes, until mushrooms and carrots are tender.

4. Add the broccoli and lemon zest, cook for an additional 2 minutes, and then add the soy sauce. Add the noodles to the wok, mix and serve.

✷ Entrée may be stored in an airtight container in the refrigerator for up to 3 days.

ZUCCHINI QUICHE

This quiche is really easy to prepare and is a great dish to make at the beginning of a busy week and keep in the fridge. Then serve this for a no-fuss dinner.

INGREDIENTS

5 medium zucchini, unpeeled, shredded and drained
2 yellow onions, finely chopped
1 cup fresh dill, finely chopped
3 tablespoons olive oil
3 eggs, beaten
3 tablespoons whole-wheat flour
1 teaspoon salt
1 teaspoon ground nutmeg
Freshly ground pepper

6 SERVINGS

SERVING SIZE: 1 slice, 210 g, 7 oz.

		% Daily Value
Calories per serving	130	
Calories from fat	60	
Total Fat	7 g	11%
Saturated Fat	1 g	4%
Cholesterol	140 mg	47%
Sodium	330 mg	14%
Total Carbohydrates	12 g	3%
Sugars	5 g	
Dietary Fiber	3 g	12%
Protein	5 g	
Vitamin A		14%
Vitamin C		30%
Calcium		6%
Iron		4%
Carbohydrate Choice	1	

EXCHANGES: 1 Vegetable, 1/2 Starch, 1/2 Fat, 1/2 Medium-Fat Meat

PREPARATION

1. Preheat oven to 375°F.

2. In a large bowl, mix together the zucchini, onions and dill.

3. In a separate bowl, mix together the olive oil, eggs, flour, salt, nutmeg and pepper.

4. Add to the vegetables and mix until well combined.

5. Lightly grease a 7-inch by 11-inch baking dish with olive oil and pour in the mixture.

6. Bake for 45 minutes, until golden. Allow to cool for 10 minutes and serve warm.

✳ Entrée may be stored in an airtight container in the refrigerator for up to 4 days.

BROCCOLI WITH ALMONDS

Broccoli is not only high in vitamin C and dietary fiber, but also contains multiple nutrients with potential anticancer properties.

INGREDIENTS

3 tablespoons almond slices
2 tablespoons butter
6 cups broccoli florets
1 garlic clove, minced
$1/2$ teaspoon salt
Freshly ground pepper

4 SERVINGS

SERVING SIZE: 1 cup, 71 g, 3$1/2$ oz.

Calories per serving	110	% Daily
Calories from fat	70	Value
Total Fat	8 g	12%
Saturated Fat	3 g	12%
Cholesterol	10 mg	3%
Sodium	235 mg	10%
Total Carbohydrates	7 g	2%
Sugars	2 g	
Dietary Fiber	3 g	11%
Protein	4 g	
Vitamin A		58%
Vitamin C		130%
Calcium		3%
Iron		5%
Carbohydrate Choice	$1/2$	
EXCHANGES: 1$1/2$ Vegetable, 1$1/2$ Fat		

PREPARATION

1. Place the almonds in a large skillet over medium heat and cook for 3 minutes, stirring frequently, until golden. Set aside for later use.

2. Heat the butter in a large skillet over medium heat, add the broccoli florets and garlic, and sauté for about 5-7 minutes, until softened. Season with salt and pepper.

3. Place on serving plate and top with toasted almonds. Serve warm.

✳ May be stored in an airtight container in the refrigerator for up to 3 days.

¤ *Broccoli with Almonds*

KOHLRABI, SPINACH & FETA QUICHE

Kohlrabi, a member of the cabbage family, is similar in taste and texture to broccoli stem or cabbage heart, but is milder and sweeter, with a higher ratio of flesh to skin.

INGREDIENTS

2 tablespoons olive oil

3 kohlrabies (about 7 oz. each), peeled and julienned

4 celery ribs, thinly sliced

2 fennel bulbs, trimmed and thinly sliced

2 large yellow onions, finely chopped

15 oz. fresh spinach leaves

4 oz. feta cheese

3 tablespoons whole-wheat flour

3 eggs, beaten

1 teaspoon salt

1 teaspoon ground nutmeg

Freshly ground pepper

10 SERVINGS

SERVING SIZE: 1 slice, 210 g, 7 oz.

Calories per serving	140	% Daily
Calories from fat	50	Value
Total Fat	6 g	9%
Saturated Fat	2 g	8%
Cholesterol	100 mg	33%
Sodium	420 mg	18%
Total Carbohydrates	13 g	4%
Sugars	4 g	
Dietary Fiber	5 g	19%
Protein	8 g	
Vitamin A		84%
Vitamin C		50%
Calcium		14%
Iron		11%

Carbohydrate Choice 1

EXCHANGES: 2 Vegetable, 1/2 Fat 1/2 Medium-Fat Meat

PREPARATION

1. Preheat oven to 400ºF.

2. Heat the olive oil in a large nonstick skillet over medium heat, add the kohlrabi, celery, fennel and onions and sauté for 10 minutes, until softened. Add the spinach and continue to cook for an additional 5 minutes. Remove from heat.

3. In a large bowl mix together the feta, whole-wheat flour, eggs, salt, nutmeg and pepper. Add the sautéed vegetables and mix until well combined.

4. Lightly grease a 7-inch by 11-inch baking dish with olive oil and pour in the mixture. Cover dish with aluminum foil and bake for 35 minutes.

5. Remove aluminum foil and bake, uncovered, for an additional 15-20 minutes, until golden. Allow to cool for 10 minutes and serve warm.

✳ Entrée may be stored in an airtight container in the refrigerator for up to 4 days.

GINGER CAULIFLOWER

Cauliflower is low in fat, but high in dietary fiber, folate, water and vitamin C. Like other members of the cabbage family, cauliflower contains several phytochemicals, which may be beneficial to our health because they help prevent certain cancers.

INGREDIENTS

1 tablespoon canola oil
1 medium yellow onion, finely chopped
1 garlic clove, minced
One 2-inch piece of fresh ginger, peeled and grated
8 cups cauliflower florets
1 teaspoon salt
1/2 cup water

6 SERVINGS

SERVING SIZE: 1 cup, 120 g, 4 oz.

		% Daily Value
Calories per serving	63	
Calories from fat	22	
Total Fat	2 g	4%
Saturated Fat	0 g	0%
Cholesterol	0 mg	0%
Sodium	429 mg	18%
Total Carbohydrates	9 g	3%
Sugars	4 g	
Dietary Fiber	4 g	8%
Protein	3 g	
Vitamin A		0%
Vitamin C		106%
Calcium		4%
Iron		4%

Carbohydrate Choice 1/2

EXCHANGES: 1/2 Vegetable, 1/2 Starch

PREPARATION

1. Heat the oil in a medium saucepan over medium heat and add the onions.

2. Sauté for about 7 minutes, until golden. Add the garlic and ginger and continue to sauté for an additional 3 minutes.

3. Add the cauliflower and continue to cook, stirring frequently, for another 5 minutes.

4. Add the salt and water, reduce heat to low and cook, uncovered, for 15-20 minutes, until the cauliflower has softened. Serve warm.

✳ May be stored in an airtight container in the refrigerator for up to 5 days.

ASIAN STIR-FRY

Stir-fry dishes are easy to make, as long as you have all the ingredients on hand. Most stir-fry dishes are prepared with an abundance of oil; this stir-fry uses less oil and tastes just as good!

INGREDIENTS

For the noodles:

$4^1/_2$ oz. broad flat rice noodles

4 cups water, boiling

For the sauce:

1 tablespoon fish sauce

2 tablespoons low-sodium soy sauce

1 tablespoon fresh lemon juice

1 teaspoon sugar substitute

For the stir-fry:

1 tablespoon canola oil

1 garlic clove, minced

One 1-inch piece fresh ginger, peeled and julienned

2 carrots, peeled and julienned

1 cup cabbage, thinly sliced

5 oz. canned bamboo shoot strips, washed and drained

$2^1/_2$ cups bean sprouts

For garnish:

2 tablespoons sesame oil

1 cup cilantro leaves, coarsely chopped

1 tablespoon black sesame seeds

6 SERVINGS

SERVING SIZE: 2 cups, 210 g, 7 oz.

		% Daily Value
Calories per serving	160	
Calories from fat	40	
Total Fat	4 g	6%
Saturated Fat	0 g	0%
Cholesterol	0 mg	0%
Sodium	360 mg	15%
Total Carbohydrates	26 g	9%
Sugars	4 g	
Dietary Fiber	4 g	15%
Protein	5 g	
Vitamin A		114%
Vitamin C		60%
Calcium		6%
Iron		8%
Carbohydrate Choice	2	

EXCHANGES: $3^1/_2$ Vegetable, $^1/_2$ Starch, $^1/_2$ Fat

PREPARATION

1. Soak the rice noodles in large bowl with boiling water and allow noodles to stand for 5 minutes. Drain and set aside for later use.

2. In a small bowl, mix together all of the sauce ingredients. Set aside for later use.

3. Heat the oil in a large wok over medium heat, add the garlic and ginger and sauté for 2-3 minutes. Add the carrots and sauté for 1 minute, and then add the cabbage and sauté for another minute. Add the bamboo shoots and bean sprouts and sauté for another 2 minutes.

4. Add the noodles and sauce to the wok and cook for 1 minute, while constantly stirring. Remove from heat, garnish with sesame oil, cilantro and sesame seeds and serve.

✱ Entrée may be stored in an airtight container in the refrigerator for up to 3 days.

ROASTED FENNEL

The delicate flavor of fennel is perfectly complemented by orange juice and cinnamon for a low calorie side dish.

INGREDIENTS

3 large fennel bulbs, trimmed and quartered
$1/2$ cup fresh orange juice
1 cup water
$1/2$ teaspoon salt
1 teaspoon dried cilantro
$1/2$ teaspoon cinnamon

6 SERVINGS

SERVING SIZE: 1 cup, 150 g, 5 oz.

		% Daily Value
Calories per serving	40	
Calories from fat	0	
Total Fat	0 g	0%
Saturated Fat	0 g	0%
Cholesterol	0 mg	0%
Sodium	195 mg	8%
Total Carbohydrates	9 g	3%
Sugars	1 g	
Dietary Fiber	3 g	12%
Protein	2 g	
Vitamin A		3%
Vitamin C		10%
Calcium		5%
Iron		5%

Carbohydrate Choice $1/2$

EXCHANGES: 2 Vegetable

PREPARATION

1. Preheat oven to 375° F.

2. Place all ingredients in a large bowl and mix until well-combined.

3. Place mixture in one layer into a large baking dish. If the fennel is not completely covered with liquid, add more water until covered.

4. Cover with aluminum foil and bake for 45 minutes. Remove aluminum foil and bake, uncovered, for an additional 15 minutes until the fennel is tender and serve.

✱ May be stored in an airtight container in the refrigerator for up to 5 days.

SWEET & SOUR TOFU

Tofu is a great source of protein in this vegetarian dish. Serve alongside basmati rice for a whole, nutritious meal.

INGREDIENTS

2 tablespoons low-sodium soy sauce
2 packets sugar substitute
3 tablespoons rice vinegar
$1/4$ teaspoon red pepper flakes (optional)
2 tablespoons Sweet Chili Sauce (see page 58)
1 tablespoon canola oil
1 medium yellow onion, finely chopped
3 garlic cloves, minced
6 oz. tofu, cut into strips
1 red bell pepper, cut into strips
1 orange bell pepper, cut into strips
3 cups snow peas (fresh or frozen and thawed)
3 cups baby corn (canned or frozen and thawed), halved diagonally

For garnish:
$1/4$ cup fresh cilantro leaves

5 SERVINGS

SERVING SIZE: 1 $1/2$ cups, 210 g, 7 oz.		
Calories per serving	110	% Daily
Calories from fat	30	Value
Total Fat	3 g	5%
Saturated Fat	0 g	0%
Cholesterol	0 mg	0%
Sodium	325 mg	14%
Total Carbohydrates	14 g	5%
Sugars	4 g	
Dietary Fiber	3 g	12%
Protein	8 g	
Vitamin A		26%
Vitamin C		159%
Calcium		9%
Iron		9%
Carbohydrate Choice	1	

EXCHANGES: $1/2$ Medium-Fat Meat, 3 Vegetable

PREPARATION

1. In a small bowl, mix together the soy sauce, sugar substitute, rice vinegar, red pepper flakes and Sweet Chili Sauce. Set aside for later use.

2. Heat the oil in a large wok over medium heat, add the onion and garlic and cook for 5-7 minutes, until softened. Add the tofu and bell peppers and continue to cook for another 2-3 minutes.

3. Add the snow peas and baby corn and cook for another minute.

4. Add sauce to wok and cook for 1 minute while constantly stirring. Garnish with cilantro and serve.

✳ May be stored in an airtight container in the refrigerator for up to 3 days.

AROMATIC RICE PILAF

This pilaf dish is inspired by Indian cuisine. Both white and brown basmati have more fiber than other types of rice. This recipe contains more than 100% of the daily recommendation of vitamin A.

INGREDIENTS

1 tablespoon olive oil
1 large yellow onion, finely chopped
1 garlic clove, thinly sliced
1 cup brown basmati rice
2 cups + $1/2$ cup water
3 carrots, peeled and shredded
1 teaspoon coarse salt
$1/2$ teaspoon cinnamon
$1/2$ teaspoon ground cardamom
$1/2$ teaspoon ground nutmeg
$1/2$ teaspoon garam masala
Grated orange zest from 1 orange

6 SERVINGS

SERVING SIZE: 1 cup, 150 g, 5 oz.

		% Daily Value
Calories per serving	110	
Calories from fat	20	
Total Fat	2 g	3%
Saturated Fat	0 g	0%
Cholesterol	0 mg	0%
Sodium	320 mg	13%
Total Carbohydrates	24 g	8%
Sugars	3 g	
Dietary Fiber	3 g	12%
Protein	2 g	
Vitamin A		126%
Vitamin C		4%
Calcium		3%
Iron		3%

Carbohydrate Choice $1^1/2$

EXCHANGES: $1^1/2$ Vegetable, 1 Starch

PREPARATION

1. Heat the oil in a medium saucepan over medium heat, add the onion and garlic and sauté for 5-7 minutes, until golden.

2. Add the rice, 2 cups of water, carrots, salt, cinnamon, cardamom, nutmeg and garam masala, mix and bring to a boil.

3. Lower heat, cover and cook for 30 minutes. Remove from heat.

4. Add the remaining $1/2$ cup water and orange zest, cover and allow rice to stand at room temperature for 10 minutes before serving. Serve warm.

✳ May be stored in an airtight container in the refrigerator for up to 5 days.

¤ *Whole-Wheat Penne in Tomato Sauce*

WHOLE-WHEAT PENNE IN TOMATO SAUCE

Kids love plain pasta in tomato sauce, making this the perfect healthy recipe when the little ones are around.

INGREDIENTS

2 cups whole-wheat penne
1 tablespoon butter
2 garlic cloves, thinly sliced
4 cups crushed tomatoes
$1/2$ cup water
3 tablespoons tomato paste
2 cups cherry tomatoes, halved
$1/4$ cup basil leaves, cut into strips
1 teaspoon salt
Freshly ground pepper

For garnish:
Whole basil leaves

5 SERVINGS

SERVING SIZE: 1 cup cooked pasta + 1 cup sauce, 300 g, 10 oz.		
Calories per serving	180	% Daily Value
Calories from fat	30	
Total Fat	3 g	4%
Saturated Fat	1 g	5%
Cholesterol	5 mg	2%
Sodium	410 mg	20%
Total Carbohydrates	31 g	10%
Sugars	8 g	
Dietary Fiber	4 g	17%
Protein	7 g	
Vitamin A		28%
Vitamin C		20%
Calcium		3%
Iron		7%
Carbohydrate Choice	2	
EXCHANGES: 2 Vegetable, 1$1/2$ Starch		

PREPARATION

1. Cook the pasta in a large saucepan filled with boiling water until *al dente* and then drain. Set aside for later use.

2. Heat the butter in a large skillet over medium heat, add the garlic and sauté for 1 minute. Add the crushed tomatoes, $1/2$ cup water and tomato paste and cook for 5 minutes.

3. Add the cherry tomatoes and basil leaves. Season with salt and pepper and cook on low heat for an additional 10 minutes, until tomatoes are soft.

4. Add the pasta to the sauce and cook for 3-5 minutes, stirring occasionally. Garnish with whole basil leaves. Serve warm.

✳ May be stored in an airtight container in the refrigerator for up to 3 days.

WHOLE-WHEAT PASTA WITH ZUCCHINI & SAGE

It has been shown that the consumption of whole grains helps to regulate glucose levels and reduce cholesterol. They also reduce the risk of heart disease and high blood pressure, both more common among people with diabetes.

INGREDIENTS

5 oz. whole-wheat spaghetti
1 tablespoon olive oil
1 large yellow onion, thinly sliced
1 garlic clove, minced
3 medium zucchini, thinly sliced
$1/4$ cup fresh sage leaves
1 teaspoon salt
Freshly ground pepper

4 SERVINGS

SERVING SIZE: 1 1/2 cups cooked pasta + vegetables, 330 g, 11 oz.

		% Daily Value
Calories per serving	200	
Calories from fat	40	
Total Fat	4 g	6%
Saturated Fat	1 g	3%
Cholesterol	0 mg	0%
Sodium	505 mg	21%
Total Carbohydrates	35 g	12%
Sugars	6 g	
Dietary Fiber	5 g	18%
Protein	7 g	
Vitamin A		6%
Vitamin C		30%
Calcium		4%
Iron		4%
Carbohydrate Choice	2 1/2	

EXCHANGES: 1 Vegetable, 2 Starch, 1/2 Fat

PREPARATION

1. Cook the pasta in a large saucepan filled with boiling water until *al dente* and then drain. Set aside for later use.

2. Heat the olive oil in a large skillet over medium heat, add the onion and sauté for about 7 minutes, until softened. Add the garlic and zucchini and cook for 15-20 minutes, until tender.

3. Remove from heat, add the whole sage leaves, season with salt and pepper and add the pasta. Return to a low heat and cook for 3-5 minutes, stirring occasionally. Serve warm.

✳ Entrée may be stored in an airtight container in the refrigerator for up to 3 days.

¤ *Couscous with Vegetables*

COUSCOUS WITH VEGETABLES

This dish calls for whole-wheat couscous, which may be difficult to find. You can replace it with regular couscous, which is filling and tasty, yet lower in fiber. The vegetables in this recipe provide well over the recommended daily intake of vitamin A.

INGREDIENTS

For the couscous:
1 cup whole-wheat couscous
2 cups boiling water
1 teaspoon salt

For the vegetables:
1 tablespoon olive oil
1 medium yellow onion, coarsely chopped
1 garlic clove, minced
1/2 pound fresh pumpkin, peeled, seeded and cut into 2-inch cubes
2 carrots, peeled and cut into 1/4-inch slices

1 cup cooked garbanzo beans
2 medium tomatoes, peeled and quartered
1/2 cup strained Chicken Broth (see page 25) or strained Vegetable Broth (see page 31)
1 cup water
1/2 teaspoon coarse salt
1 teaspoon turmeric
1/2 teaspoon cumin
1/2 teaspoon cinnamon
Freshly ground pepper
1 medium zucchini, cut into 1/4-inch slices

6 SERVINGS

SERVING SIZE: 1/2 cup cooked couscous + 1 cup sauce, 300 g, 10 oz.

		% Daily Value
Calories per serving	190	
Calories from fat	30	
Total Fat	3 g	5%
Saturated Fat	0 g	0%
Cholesterol	0 mg	0%
Sodium	310 mg	13%
Total Carbohydrates	34 g	11%
Sugars	4 g	
Dietary Fiber	5 g	21%
Protein	7 g	
Vitamin A		143%
Vitamin C		20%
Calcium		6%
Iron		12%

Carbohydrate Choice   2

EXCHANGES: 2 Vegetable, 1 1/2 Starch, 1/2 Fat

PREPARATION

1. Place the couscous in a large bowl and cover with boiling water. Add salt, mix and cover. Let the couscous stand, covered for 15-20 minutes, until softened. Set aside for later use.

2. Heat olive oil in a large saucepan over medium heat, add the onion and garlic and sauté for 5-7 minutes, until softened.

3. Add the pumpkin, carrots, garbanzo beans, tomatoes, broth, water, salt, turmeric, cumin, cinnamon and ground pepper. Cook for 30 minutes, until vegetables are tender.

4. Add the zucchini and cook for an additional 15 minutes. Serve couscous with warm vegetables.

✳ May be stored in an airtight container in the refrigerator for up to 3 days.

QUINOA ANTIPASTI

This vegetable-packed dish provides the entire recommended daily intake of vitamin C and is rich in vitamin A, calcium, and iron. One serving provides a full 6 grams of fiber!

INGREDIENTS

1 red bell pepper, cut into strips

1 green bell pepper, cut into strips

2 medium zucchini, sliced thinly, lengthwise

3 cups cauliflower florets

1 tablespoon olive oil

1 large onion, finely chopped

2 celery ribs, finely chopped

2 carrots, peeled and finely chopped

1 cup quinoa, washed thoroughly and drained

1 cup strained Vegetable Broth (see page 31)

1 cup water

2 tablespoons low-sodium soy sauce

$^1/_2$ cup sesame tahini

8 SERVINGS

SERVING SIZE: 1 cup cooked quinoa + 1 cup vegetables, 300 g, 10 oz.

		% Daily Value
Calories per serving	250	
Calories from fat	110	
Total Fat	12 g	19%
Saturated Fat	2 g	8%
Cholesterol	0 mg	0%
Sodium	200 mg	8%
Total Carbohydrates	28 g	9%
Sugars	3 g	
Dietary Fiber	6 g	24%
Protein	9 g	
Vitamin A		100%
Vitamin C		100%
Calcium		15%
Iron		22%

Carbohydrate Choice   2

EXCHANGES: 2$^1/_2$ Vegetable, 1 Starch, 2$^1/_2$ Fat

PREPARATION

1. Preheat oven to 375ºF. Place bell peppers, zucchini and cauliflower on a baking sheet lined with parchment paper and drizzle with olive oil. Bake for 30 minutes, until vegetables are tender. Keep warm for later use.

2. Meanwhile, prepare the quinoa: Spray a medium saucepan with cooking oil, heat over medium heat and add the onions. Sauté for about 7 minutes, until golden. Add the celery and carrots and continue to cook for an additional 5-7 minutes, until softened.

3. Add the quinoa, vegetable broth and water and cook on low heat, uncovered, for about 30 minutes, until all the liquid is absorbed. Remove from heat and add the soy sauce and mix until combined. Place quinoa on a large serving plate and top with roasted vegetables. Drizzle with tahini and serve.

✱ May be stored in an airtight container in the refrigerator for up to 3 days.

POTATO & CELERY STEW

This recipe works great as a hearty side dish when serving chicken or beef. Try it with the Drumsticks with Orange Juice & Fennel (see page 112) or with the Baked Kabobs (see page 124).

INGREDIENTS

5 celery ribs, coarsely chopped

1 celeriac, peeled and cut into $^1/_2$-inch cubes

2 medium russet potatoes, peeled and cut into $^1/_2$-inch cubes

$^1/_3$ cup fresh lemon juice

1$^1/_2$ cups strained Chicken Broth (see page 25)

1 teaspoon salt

1 teaspoon cumin

$^1/_2$ teaspoon ground allspice

8 SERVINGS

PREPARATION

1. Place all ingredients in a large saucepan over high heat and bring to a boil.

2. Reduce heat, cover and cook for 20 minutes, until the potatoes are tender. Serve warm.

* May be stored in an airtight container in the refrigerator for up to 5 days.

SERVING SIZE: 1 cup, 150 g, 5 oz.

		% Daily Value
Calories per serving	70	
Calories from fat	10	
Total Fat	1 g	1%
Saturated Fat	0 g	0%
Cholesterol	0 mg	0%
Sodium	160 mg	7%
Total Carbohydrates	13 g	4%
Sugars	2 g	
Dietary Fiber	2 g	8%
Protein	4 g	
Vitamin A		4%
Vitamin C		10%
Calcium		2%
Iron		6%
Carbohydrate Choice	1	

EXCHANGES: 1 Vegetable, $^1/_2$ Starch

¤ *Brown Rice with Swiss Chard & Spinach*

BROWN RICE WITH SWISS CHARD & SPINACH

Brown rice is much more nutritious than its regular, white rice counterpart. Brown rice is a better source of dietary fiber, vitamins and minerals than white rice.

INGREDIENTS

1 tablespoon olive oil

1 large onion, finely chopped

3 garlic cloves, minced

1 bunch Swiss chard, ribs cut crosswise into 1-inch pieces, leaves torn into 2-inch pieces

5 cups fresh spinach leaves

$1/2$ cup fresh dill, finely chopped

$3/4$ cup short grain brown rice

1 teaspoon coarse salt

$1^1/2$ cups water

3 tablespoons fresh lemon juice

6 SERVINGS

SERVING SIZE: 1 cup, 210 g, 7 oz.		
Calories per serving	110	% Daily
Calories from fat	10	Value
Total Fat	1 g	1%
Saturated Fat	0 g	0%
Cholesterol	0 mg	0%
Sodium	420 mg	18%
Total Carbohydrates	20 g	7%
Sugars	2 g	
Dietary Fiber	3 g	12%
Protein	4 g	
Vitamin A		138%
Vitamin C		10%
Calcium		8%
Iron		6%
Carbohydrate Choice	$1^1/2$	
EXCHANGES: 1 Vegetable, 1 Starch		

PREPARATION

1. Heat the olive oil in a medium saucepan, add the onion and garlic and sauté for 5 minutes, until softened. Add the Swiss chard, spinach and dill and continue to cook for an additional 5 minutes.

2. Add the rice, salt and water, mix and bring to a boil. Reduce heat, cover and cook for 30 minutes. Remove from heat and keep covered for another 5 minutes.

3. Mix in the lemon juice and serve warm.

✳ May be stored in an airtight container in the refrigerator for up to 3 days.

INDIAN RICE

This is a great rice dish which can stand alone or be served as part of a whole meal, especially when entertaining. I recommend serving this with Turkey Curry (see page 115), as the combination of the two makes for a complete wholesome meal. Place the rice into small individual bowls and have each guest help themselves with their preferred toppings.

INGREDIENTS

3$^1/_2$ cups water
1$^1/_2$ cups brown basmati rice
4 large tomatoes, coarsely chopped
2 small cucumbers, peeled and coarsely chopped
4 bananas, sliced into $^1/_2$-inch slices
1 mango, peeled and cut into $^1/_2$-inch cubes
3 kiwis, peeled and thinly sliced
$^1/_4$ cup fresh lemon juice
1 oz. roasted peanuts, coarsely chopped

10 SERVINGS

SERVING SIZE: $^1/_2$ cup rice + 1$^1/_2$ cups fruits and vegetables, 300 g, 10 oz.

		% Daily Value
Calories per serving	180	
Calories from fat	20	
Total Fat	2 g	3%
Saturated Fat	1 g	4%
Cholesterol	0 mg	0%
Sodium	15 mg	1%
Total Carbohydrates	37 g	12%
Sugars	15 g	
Dietary Fiber	4 g	16%
Protein	4 g	
Vitamin A		16%
Vitamin C		85%
Calcium		3%
Iron		4%
Carbohydrate Choice	**2$^1/_2$**	

EXCHANGES: 1 Vegetable, 1 Starch, 1 Fruit, $^1/_2$ Fat

PREPARATION

1. Boil the water in a medium saucepan and add the rice. Cook, covered, for 20 minutes on low heat. Keep covered, remove from heat and allow rice to stand for an additional 5 minutes.

2. Arrange the tomatoes, cucumbers, bananas, mangos and kiwi on a large serving platter. Sprinkle the lemon juice over the fruit to prevent browning.

3. Place the roasted peanuts into a small bowl and place onto the platter.

4. Place rice into individual serving bowls and serve with the fruits and vegetables.

SWISS CHARD, BELL PEPPER & FETA CHEESE QUICHE

This quiche is rich in vitamins and minerals. This one is prepared without the calorie-filled crust usually found in most quiches.

INGREDIENTS

1 tablespoon olive oil
4 red bell peppers, cut into 1/4-inch strips
4 Swiss chard leaves, coarsely chopped
1/2 cup basil leaves, finely chopped
1/4 cup water
3 oz. feta cheese, cut into small cubes
2 tablespoons bread crumbs
1 cup low-fat plain yogurt
3 eggs
1 tablespoon salt
1/2 teaspoon grated nutmeg
Freshly ground pepper

8 SERVINGS

SERVING SIZE: 1 slice, 180 g, 6 oz.

Calories per serving	120	% Daily
Calories from fat	60	Value
Total Fat	7 g	10%
Saturated Fat	3 g	14%
Cholesterol	120 mg	40%
Sodium	755 mg	31%
Total Carbohydrates	10 g	3%
Sugars	5 g	
Dietary Fiber	2 g	7%
Protein	7 g	
Vitamin A		107%
Vitamin C		78%
Calcium		15%
Iron		12%

Carbohydrate Choice   1/2

EXCHANGES: 2 Vegetable, 1/2 Fat,
1/2 Medium-Fat Meat

PREPARATION

1. Preheat oven to 400°F. Heat the olive oil in a large pan on medium heat and add the bell peppers. Sauté for 10-12 minutes, until softened.

2. Add the Swiss chard, basil leaves and water and continue to cook for 5-7 minutes, until softened. Remove from heat, add the feta cheese and stir to combine.

3. Grease a 9-inch round baking pan and evenly coat with bread crumbs. Pour the cooked vegetable and feta mix into the baking pan.

4. In a medium bowl, mix together the yogurt, eggs, salt, nutmeg and pepper until well combined. Evenly pour mixture over the vegetables.

5. Bake for 25-30 minutes, until center of quiche is set. Serve warm or at room temperature.

✱ May be stored in the refrigerator for up to 4 days.

DESSERTS

✠ Fruit Salad with Homemade Berry Sauce

FRUIT SALAD WITH HOMEMADE BERRY SAUCE

Fruit salad is an easy, festive dish for a summer dessert. Use ripe fruit that's in season for the best results. People with diabetes should consider the large amount of natural sugar in this recipe.

4 SERVINGS

SERVING SIZE: 1 1/2 cups, 120 g, 4 oz.

		% Daily
Calories per serving	60	Value
Calories from fat	0	
Total Fat	0 g	0%
Saturated Fat	0 g	0%
Cholesterol	0 mg	0%
Sodium	5 mg	0%
Total Carbohydrates	15 g	5%
Sugars	12 g	
Dietary Fiber	2 g	8%
Protein	1 g	
Vitamin A		3%
Vitamin C		56%
Calcium		1%
Iron		2%
Carbohydrate Choice	**1**	
EXCHANGES: 1 Fruit		

INGREDIENTS

2 kiwi fruits, peeled and thinly sliced
1 medium pear, cut into 1/4-inch slices
1 large peach, cut into 1/4-inch slices
1 packet sugar substitute
1/4 cup Homemade Berry Sauce (see page 158)

PREPARATION

1. Place kiwi, pear, peach and sugar substitute in a large serving bowl and mix. Allow to stand at room temperature for 5 minutes.

2. Add the berry sauce and serve immediately.

HOMEMADE BERRY SAUCE

You can make this sauce using any type of berries you prefer: blueberries, blackberries, strawberries, raspberries, cranberries or a mix. This is a great sauce to make and keep in the fridge to jazz up any dessert, or even to serve over fresh fruit.

INGREDIENTS

2 cups fresh or frozen berries
2 cups water
1 tablespoon fresh lemon juice
2 packets sugar substitute
2 tablespoons cornstarch

8 SERVINGS

SERVING SIZE: 1/4 cup, 60 g, 2 oz.

		% Daily Value
Calories per serving	30	
Calories from fat	0	
Total Fat	0 g	0%
Saturated Fat	0 g	0%
Cholesterol	0 mg	0%
Sodium	5 mg	0%
Total Carbohydrates	6 g	2%
Sugars	5 g	
Dietary Fiber	1 g	4%
Protein	0 g	
Vitamin A		1%
Vitamin C		8%
Calcium		1%
Iron		2%

Carbohydrate Choice 1/2

EXCHANGES: 1/2 Fruit

PREPARATION

1. Place the berries, 1 1/2 cups of the water, lemon juice and sugar substitute in a medium saucepan and bring to a boil over high heat.

2. In a small bowl, mix the cornstarch with the remaining 1/2 cup of water and stir into the berry mixture. Stir frequently until the sauce has thickened, about 4-5 minutes. Remove from heat and cool.

3. Store in an airtight container in the refrigerator until ready to serve.

✳ May be stored in an airtight jar in the refrigerator for up to 1 month.

FRUIT SALAD SOUFFLÉ

For this recipe, I use peaches and plums, which are at their peak during the summer. If you are making this recipe during the winter months, simply substitute with apples and bananas for maximum flavor. People with diabetes should consider the large amount of natural sugar in the fruit.

INGREDIENTS

2 peaches, sliced

4 plums, sliced

¼ cup fresh lemon juice

2 packets sugar substitute

½ teaspoon cinnamon

1 tablespoon brandy

1 egg, separated

3 SERVINGS

SERVING SIZE: 1 cup, 210 g, 4 oz.

		% Daily Value
Calories per serving	130	
Calories from fat	30	
Total Fat	3 g	4%
Saturated Fat	1 g	4%
Cholesterol	110 mg	37%
Sodium	45 mg	2%
Total Carbohydrates	22 g	7%
Sugars	18 g	
Dietary Fiber	3 g	12%
Protein	4 g	
Vitamin A		15%
Vitamin C		32%
Calcium		2%
Iron		4%
Carbohydrate Choice	**1½**	

EXCHANGES: ½ **Medium-Fat Meat,**
1½ **Fruit**

PREPARATION

1. Preheat oven to 425ºF.

2. In a large bowl, mix together peaches, plums, lemon juice, 1 packet of the sugar substitute, cinnamon and brandy. Let it stand at room temperature for 5 minutes.

3. In a separate bowl, whisk together the egg white with the remaining 1 packet of sugar substitute. Fold in the egg yolk and mix carefully until mixture is smooth.

4. Place the fruit mixture into a baking dish and pour the egg mixture over the fruit. Bake for 10 minutes, until golden. Serve warm.

COFFEE BAVARIAN CREAM WITH CARAMELIZED WALNUTS

This classic dessert is typically filled with calories, but this festive version is just as delicious with not nearly the amount of calories.

5 SERVINGS

SERVING SIZE: 1 cup, 100 g, 3¹/₂ oz.

Calories per serving	100	% Daily
Calories from fat	40	Value
Total Fat	4 g	7%
Saturated Fat	1 g	4%
Cholesterol	60 mg	20%
Sodium	100 mg	4%
Total Carbohydrates	8 g	3%
Sugars	6 g	
Dietary Fiber	1 g	0%
Protein	6 g	
Vitamin A		1%
Vitamin C		1%
Calcium		7%
Iron		2%

Carbohydrate Choice ¹/₂

EXCHANGES: ¹/₂ Medium-Fat Meat, ¹/₂ Low-fat Milk

INGREDIENTS

For the caramelized walnuts:
1 tablespoon honey
3 tablespoons walnuts, finely chopped

For the Bavarian cream:
1 envelope unflavored gelatin
¹/₂ cup cold water

1 egg, separated + 1 egg white
4 packets sugar substitute
Pinch of salt
1 cup reduced-fat (2%) milk
2 teaspoons instant coffee granules, dissolved in ¹/₂ cup boiling water
2 tablespoons cornstarch, dissolved in ¹/₂ cup cold water
1 tablespoon brandy

PREPARATION

1. Place the honey and chopped walnuts in a small saucepan over medium heat and caramelize for 2-3 minutes. Pour the mixture onto a piece of parchment paper, and allow it to cool to room temperature.

2. Sprinkle gelatin over ¹/₂ cup cold water and let stand 5 minutes.

3. Using a stand mixer fitted with a whisk attachment, whisk together the 2 egg whites with the sugar substitute on high speed for about 1-2 minutes, until soft peaks form. Add the salt and whisk for another minute. Set aside.

4. In the top of a double boiler, whisk the milk, egg yolk, dissolved coffee and dissolved cornstarch over simmering water. Whisking constantly, cook until thickened, about 7 minutes. Gradually add the gelatin mixture and brandy, whisking until mixture is smooth. Remove the top of double boiler from heat. Whisking constantly, gradually add egg whites. Return top of double boiler to simmering water. Whisking constantly, cook until mixture reaches 160°F. Allow to cool.

5. Pour into 5 wine glasses. Chill until firm.

6. Garnish with caramelized walnuts and serve.

✳ May be stored in an airtight container in the refrigerator for up to 3 days.

¤ *Coffee Bavarian Cream with Caramelized Walnuts*

HOMEMADE STRAWBERRY ICE CREAM

This delicious ice cream is packed with flavor, but without the calories of regular ice cream.

INGREDIENTS

2/3 cup fat-free evaporated milk
4 cups fresh, whole strawberries, hulled
6 packets sugar substitute
1 teaspoon fresh lemon juice
1 teaspoon vanilla extract

10 SERVINGS

SERVING SIZE: 1/2 cup, 75 g, 2 oz.

		% Daily Value
Calories per serving	34	
Calories from fat	0	
Total Fat	0 g	0%
Saturated Fat	0 g	0%
Cholesterol	0 mg	0%
Sodium	19 mg	1%
Total Carbohydrates	7 g	2%
Sugars	5 g	
Dietary Fiber	1 g	5%
Protein	2 g	
Vitamin A		1%
Vitamin C		57%
Calcium		6%
Iron		2%

Carbohydrate Choice 1/2

EXCHANGES: 1/2 Fruit

PREPARATION

1. Place evaporated milk and beaters from an electric mixer into a mixing bowl. Freeze for 20 minutes or until ice crystals form in milk around edge of bowl.

2. Place the strawberries, sugar substitute and lemon juice in a food processor fitted with a metal blade and process until blended. Place in freezer to chill.

3. Using an electric mixer and chilled beaters, beat evaporated milk 1 minute, until frothy. Add vanilla and beat until stiff peaks form, about 2 minutes.

4. Fold beaten milk mixture into chilled strawberry mixture. Cover with plastic wrap and freeze for at least 5 hours before serving.

5. Serve ice cream in individual serving dishes.

✳ May be stored in an airtight container in the freezer for up to 2 months.

PEARS
IN
RED WINE

This simple, yet elegant dessert is easy to make and is an impressive way to serve fruit. People with diabetes should consider the large amount of sugar in this recipe.

INGREDIENTS

¹/₂ cup dry red wine

2 cups water

2 cinnamon sticks

4 whole cloves

¹/₂ cup raspberries

2 packets sugar substitute

1 tablespoon honey

8 small pears, peeled, stems intact

8 SERVINGS

SERVING SIZE: 1 pear + sauce, 200 g, 7 oz.

		% Daily Value
Calories per serving	110	
Calories from fat	0	
Total Fat	0 g	0%
Saturated Fat	0 g	0%
Cholesterol	0 mg	0%
Sodium	5 mg	0%
Total Carbohydrates	27 g	9%
Sugars	17 g	
Dietary Fiber	7 g	29%
Protein	1 g	
Vitamin A		1%
Vitamin C		16%
Calcium		1%
Iron		1%
Carbohydrate Choice	2	

EXCHANGES: 2 Fruit

PREPARATION

1. Place the wine, water, cinnamon sticks, cloves, raspberries, sugar substitute and honey in a large saucepan and cook over medium heat for 5 minutes.

2. Add the pears and bring to a boil. Lower heat and cook, uncovered, for about 20 minutes, or until pears are soft but still hold their shape.

3. Remove the pears from the saucepan and set aside. Continue to cook the sauce over low heat, until slightly reduced.

4. Serve pears with sauce.

✳ May be stored in an airtight container in the refrigerator for up to 5 days.

¤ *Pears in Red Wine*

PEACHES IN CUSTARD

Peaches are at their peak during the summer months, making this a perfect dessert to serve at a summer outdoor barbecue.

INGREDIENTS

2 large firm peaches, halved and pitted

1 $^1/_2$ tablespoons cornstarch

$^1/_2$ cup water

1 egg yolk

1 cup reduced-fat (2%) milk

1 teaspoon pure vanilla extract

3 packets sugar substitute

For garnish:

$^1/_2$ cup fresh berries (blueberries, raspberries, blackberries, etc.)

1 teaspoon cinnamon

4 SERVINGS

SERVING SIZE: $^1/_2$ peach + $^1/_2$ cup sauce, 180 g, 6 oz.

		% Daily Value
Calories per serving	100	
Calories from fat	20	
Total Fat	3 g	4%
Saturated Fat	1 g	3%
Cholesterol	25 mg	8%
Sodium	30 mg	1%
Total Carbohydrates	16 g	5%
Sugars	9 g	
Dietary Fiber	3 g	11%
Protein	3 g	
Vitamin A		7%
Vitamin C		20%
Calcium		9%
Iron		2%

Carbohydrate Choice 1

EXCHANGES: 1 Fruit, $^1/_2$ Medium-Fat Meat

PREPARATION

1. Preheat oven to 350°F.

2. Place peaches, cut side down, into a baking dish and bake for 10 minutes. Allow to cool for 5 minutes, and then carefully remove skins. Set aside peaches for later use.

3. In a small bowl, mix together the cornstarch, water and egg yolk until cornstarch is completely dissolved. Set aside.

4. Heat the milk and vanilla extract in a saucepan over medium heat until simmering. Gradually add the cornstarch mixture while constantly whisking, until thickened. Add sugar substitute and continue whisking for another minute. Remove from heat.

5. Place the peaches in individual serving dishes, top with warm custard and garnish with a few berries and cinnamon.

✳ May be stored in an airtight container in the refrigerator for up to 3 days.

BAKED APPLES WITH CRANBERRY SAUCE

Cranberries are rich in dietary fiber and are a good source of anti-oxidants, which are known to not only fight cancer, but also benefit the cardiovascular and immune systems. Research suggests that apples may reduce the risk of certain cancers, such as colon, prostate and lung cancer. This dessert contains dietary fiber and antioxidants, making it a healthy and tasty option to finish a meal.

INGREDIENTS

4 Granny Smith apples, peeled, cored and sliced into $1/4$-inch slices
$1/4$ cup walnuts, coarsely chopped

For the sauce:
8 oz. cranberries
$2^1/_2$ cups water
1 tablespoon honey
4 packets sugar substitute
$1^1/_2$ tablespoons cornstarch

8 SERVINGS

SERVING SIZE: $^1/_2$ apple + $^1/_2$ cup sauce, 120 g, 4 oz.		
Calories per serving	60	% Daily
Calories from fat	20	Value
Total Fat	2 g	3%
Saturated Fat	0 g	0%
Cholesterol	0 mg	0%
Sodium	0 mg	0%
Total Carbohydrates	13 g	4%
Sugars	7 g	
Dietary Fiber	3 g	12%
Protein	1 g	
Vitamin A		1%
Vitamin C		12%
Calcium		1%
Iron		1%
Carbohydrate Choice	1	
EXCHANGES: 1 Fruit		

PREPARATION

1. Place the cranberries in a food processor fitted with a metal blade and process until blended.

2. Place the cranberries, 2 cups of the water, honey and sugar substitute in a medium saucepan and bring to a boil over high heat.

3. In a small bowl, mix the cornstarch with the remaining $^1/_2$ cup of water and add to the berry mixture. Stir constantly until the sauce has thickened, about 3-5 minutes. Set aside for later use.

4. Preheat oven to 375ºF. Arrange apple slices in a baking dish. Pour over 2 cups of cranberry sauce and bake for 20 minutes, until apples are tender. Garnish with chopped walnuts and serve with warm or cold sauce.

✷ May be stored in an airtight container in the refrigerator for up to 5 days.

¤ *Mini Blueberry Muffins*

MINI BLUEBERRY MUFFINS

Research has shown that blueberries contain chemicals which may: inhibit cancer cell development; alleviate cognitive decline resulting from Alzheimer's; maintain healthy blood pressure and lower cholesterol. Serve with Homemade Berry Sauce (see page 158) for an exciting dessert.

INGREDIENTS

$1^1/_2$ cups whole-wheat flour
1 tablespoon baking powder
6 packets sugar substitute
$^1/_4$ cup canola oil
2 eggs
1 Granny Smith apple, peeled, cored and shredded
$^1/_4$ cup water
1 tablespoon fresh lemon juice
1 cup blueberries

30 MUFFINS

SERVING SIZE: 2 mini muffins, 22 g each, about $^2/_3$ oz.		
Calories per serving	70	% Daily
Calories from fat	10	Value
Total Fat	1 g	2%
Saturated Fat	0 g	0%
Cholesterol	40 mg	13%
Sodium	115 mg	5%
Total Carbohydrates	12 g	4%
Sugars	2 g	
Dietary Fiber	2 g	8%
Protein	3 g	
Vitamin A		1%
Vitamin C		3%
Calcium		1%
Iron		3%
Carbohydrate Choice	1	
EXCHANGES: $^1/_2$ Starch, $^1/_2$ Fruit		

PREPARATION

1. Preheat oven to 350ºF. Spray a mini muffin tin with cooking spray.

2. In a large bowl, mix together the flour, baking powder and sugar substitute. In a separate bowl, mix together the oil, eggs, apple, water and lemon juice. Stir in flour mixture.

3. Stir in blueberries.

4. Spoon batter into prepared muffin tin, filling each cup $^3/_4$ full.

5. Bake for 12-15 minutes, until golden. Allow to cool for 10 minutes before serving.

✳ May be stored in an airtight container in the freezer for up to 2 months.

CHESTNUT & WALNUT COOKIES

Sometimes a cookie is what you really need to accompany a cup of tea or coffee. These cookies are a delicious option when that need kicks in. Chestnuts, unlike other nuts and seeds, are relatively low in calories. They contain less fat, but are rich in minerals, vitamins and phytonutrients that benefit health. They are also a good source of dietary fiber and are exceptionally rich in vitamin C and folate.

30 COOKIES

SERVING SIZE: 2 cookies, 20 g, ²/₃ oz.		
Calories per serving	110	% Daily
Calories from fat	70	Value
Total Fat	8 g	13%
Saturated Fat	3 g	12%
Cholesterol	10 mg	3%
Sodium	50 mg	2%
Total Carbohydrates	9 g	3%
Sugars	0 g	
Dietary Fiber	4 g	16%
Protein	2 g	
Vitamin A		2%
Vitamin C		5%
Calcium		1%
Iron		2%
Carbohydrate Choice	¹/₂	
EXCHANGES: ¹/₂ Starch, 1¹/₂ Fat		

INGREDIENTS

4 oz. peeled chestnuts
¹/₂ cup walnuts
5 tablespoons butter
4 packets sugar substitute
1 egg white
¹/₄ cup water
³/₄ cup whole-wheat flour
¹/₂ teaspoon salt

PREPARATION

1. Preheat oven to 400ºF. Place chestnuts and walnuts in a food processor fitted with a metal blade and process until coarsely ground.

2. Using a stand mixer fitted with a whisk attachment, whisk together the butter and sugar substitute on medium speed until fluffy. Add the egg white and continue to whisk for an additional 2 minutes. Add the water and continue to whisk for an additional 2 minutes.

3. Add the flour, salt and ground nuts and continue to whisk until mixture is smooth. Using wet hands make 30 small balls, about one rounded teaspoonful, and place 1 inch apart on the baking sheet. Use the back of the spoon to slightly flatten each cookie.

4. Bake for 15-17 minutes, until golden.

＊ May be stored in an airtight container at room temperature for up to 2 weeks.

APPLE MOUSSE

This recipe literally takes 10 minutes to prepare. It's perfect as a healthy, tasty snack when you're in need of something sweet.

INGREDIENTS

2 egg whites (see Note below)
4 packets sugar substitute
2 tablespoons fresh lemon juice
2 cups sugar-free apple sauce, chilled
$1/2$ teaspoon cinnamon
Pinch of ground cloves

6 SERVINGS

SERVING SIZE: $1/2$ **cup, 90 g, 3 oz.**

		% Daily Value
Calories per serving	40	
Calories from fat	0	
Total Fat	0 g	0%
Saturated Fat	0 g	0%
Cholesterol	0 mg	0%
Sodium	25 mg	1%
Total Carbohydrates	10 g	3%
Sugars	7 g	
Dietary Fiber	1 g	4%
Protein	1 g	
Vitamin A		1%
Vitamin C		10%
Calcium		1%
Iron		1%

Carbohydrate Choice $1/2$

EXCHANGES: $1/2$ Fruit

PREPARATION

1. Using a stand mixer fitted with a whisk attachment, whisk the egg whites and sugar substitute until firm. Add 1 tablespoon of lemon juice and continue to whisk for another minute.

2. Fold in the apple sauce, remaining tablespoon lemon juice, cinnamon and cloves, until smooth.

3. Serve immediately in individual glasses.

Note: Eating raw eggs carries a risk of foodborne illness. It is safe to use pasteurized eggs or egg substitutes in dishes that won't be cooked.

PEACH UPSIDE-DOWN CAKE

This sugar-free cake is best when served right out of the oven. The peaches can be replaced with any other stone fruit such as plums or apricots.

12 SERVINGS

SERVING SIZE: 1 slice + sauce, 140 g, 5 oz.		
Calories per serving	155	% Daily
Calories from fat	53	Value
Total Fat	6 g	10%
Saturated Fat	1 g	7%
Cholesterol	36 mg	12%
Sodium	57 mg	2%
Total Carbohydrates	23 g	8%
Sugars	9 g	
Dietary Fiber	2 g	9%
Protein	4 g	
Vitamin A		6%
Vitamin C		10%
Calcium		5%
Iron		6%
Carbohydrate Choice	1 1/2	
EXCHANGES: 1 Fruit, 1 Fat, 1/2 Starch		

INGREDIENTS

4 medium peaches, cut into 1/2-inch slices
1/4 cup canola oil
1/3 cup reduced-fat (2%) milk
2 eggs
1 teaspoon pure vanilla extract
1 tablespoon fresh lemon juice
4 packets sugar substitute
3/4 cup all-purpose flour
3/4 cup whole wheat flour
1 teaspoon baking powder

For the sauce:
2 peaches, peeled, cut into 1/2-inch slices
2 tablespoons fresh or frozen raspberries
1 cup water
2 packets sugar substitute
1 tablespoon cornstarch, dissolved in 1/2 cup water

PREPARATION

1. Preheat oven to 350°F.

2. Grease a 9-inch round baking pan. Place the peach slices on the bottom of the pan in a circle pattern.

3. Using a stand mixer fitted with whisk attachment, whisk together the oil, milk, eggs, vanilla extract, lemon juice and sugar substitute on medium speed for 5 minutes, until well combined.

4. In a separate bowl, mix together both flours and baking powder. Reduce the mixer speed to low and add the flour mixture to the wet ingredients. Whisk for 2 minutes, until ingredients are just combined.

5. Pour the batter onto the peach slices and bake for 25-30 minutes, until golden and firm. Allow to cool for 10 minutes before serving.

6. Meanwhile, prepare the sauce: Place the peach slices, raspberries, water and sugar substitute in a small saucepan and cook over medium heat until boiling. Reduce heat, add the dissolved cornstarch and cook on low heat, stirring constantly, for an additional 5-7 minutes, until thickened.

7. Invert cake onto a serving plate and serve warm, with sauce.

EXCHANGE LISTS FOR DIABETES

THE FOOD LISTS

The following chart shows the amount of nutrients in 1 serving from each list.

Food List	Carbohydrates (grams)	Protein (grams)	Fat (grams)	Calories
CARBOHYDRATES				
STARCH BREAD, CEREALS & GRAINS, STARCHY VEGETABLES, CRACKERS & SNACKS, BEANS, PEAS & LENTILS	15	0 - 3	0 - 1	80
FRUITS	15	—	—	60
MILK				
FAT-FREE OR LOW-FAT (1%)	12	8	0 - 3	100
REDUCED-FAT (2%)	12	8	5	120
WHOLE	12	8	8	160
SWEETS, DESSERTS & OTHER CARBOHYDRATES	15	varies	varies	varies
NONSTARCHY VEGETABLES	5	2	—	25
MEAT & MEAT SUBSTITUTES				
LEAN	—	7	0 - 3	45
MEDIUM-FAT	—	7	4 - 7	75
HIGH-FAT	—	7	8+	100
PLANT-BASED PROTEINS	varies	7	varies	varies
FATS	—	—	5	45
ALCOHOL (1 ALCOHOL EQUIVALENT)	varies	—	—	100

STARCH

Food List	Serving Size
BAGEL, large, about 4 oz.	¼ (1 oz.)
☻BISCUIT, 2½ inches across	1
BREAD White, Whole Grain, Pumpernickel, Rye, Unfrosted Raisin ☺Reduced-calorie	 1 slice (1 oz.) 2 slices (1½ oz.)
CHAPATTI, small, 6 inches across	1
☻CORNBREAD, 1¾-inch cube	1 (1½ oz.)
ENGLISH MUFFIN	½
HOT DOG BUN / HAMBURGER BUN	½ (1 oz.)
NAAN, 8 x 2 inches	¼
PANCAKE, 4 inches across	1
PITA, 6 inches across	½
ROLL, plain, small	1 (1 oz.)
☻STUFFING, bread	⅓ cup
☻TACO SHELL, 5 inches across	2
TORTILLA, CORN, 6 inches across	1
TORTILLA, FLOUR, 6 inches across	1
TORTILLA, FLOUR, 10 inches across	⅓ tortilla
☻WAFFLE, 4 inches across	1

☺ More than 3 grams dietary fiber per serving

☻ Extra fat, or prepared with added fat (count as 1 Starch + 1 Fat).

✎ 480 milligrams or more of sodium per servng

CEREALS & GRAINS

Food List	Serving Size
BARLEY, cooked	$^1/_3$ cup
BRAN, dry	
☺ Oat	$^1/_4$ cup
☺ Wheat	$^1/_2$ cup
☺ BULGUR, cooked	$^1/_2$ cup
CEREALS	
☺ Bran	$^1/_2$ cup
Cooked (oats, oatmeal)	$^1/_2$ cup
Puffed	$1^1/_2$ cups
Shredded Wheat (plain)	$^1/_2$ cup
Sugar-coated	$^1/_2$ cup
Unsweetened	$^3/_4$ cup
COUSCOUS	$^1/_3$ cup
☹ GRANOLA	$^1/_4$ cup
Low-fat	$^1/_4$ cup
GRITS, cooked	$^1/_2$ cup
KASHA	$^1/_2$ cup
MILLET, cooked	$^1/_3$ cup
MUESLI	$^1/_4$ cup
PASTA, cooked	$^1/_3$ cup
POLENTA, cooked	$^1/_3$ cup
QUINOA, cooked	$^1/_3$ cup
RICE, white or brown, cooked	$^1/_3$ cup
TABBOULEH, cooked	$^1/_2$ cup
WHEAT GERM, dry	3 tablespoons
WILD RICE, cooked	$^1/_2$ cup

STARCHY VEGETABLES

Food List	Serving Size
CASSAVA	$^1/_3$ cup
CORN, on cob, large	$^1/_2$ cup
☺ HOMINY, canned	$^3/_4$ cup
☺ MIXED VEGETABLES With Corn, Peas or Pasta	1 cup
☺ PARSNIPS	$^1/_2$ cup
☺ PEAS, green	$^1/_2$ cup
PLANTAIN, ripe	$^1/_3$ cup
POTATO	
Baked with skin	$^1/_4$ large (3 oz.)
Boiled, all kinds	$^1/_2$ cup (3 oz.)
☹ Mashed, with Milk & Fat	$^1/_2$ cup
French-fried (Oven-baked)	1 cup (2 oz.)
☺ PUMPKIN, canned, no sugar added	1 cup
SPAGHETTI / PASTA SAUCE	$^1/_2$ cup
☺ SQUASH, winter Acorn, Butternut	1 cup
☺ SUCCOTASH	$^1/_2$ cup
YAM, SWEET POTATO, plain	$^1/_2$ cup

CRACKERS & SNACKS

Food List	Serving Size
ANIMAL CRACKERS	8
CRACKERS	
☹ Round-butter type	6
Saltine-type	6
☹ Sandwich-style, cheese or peanut butter filling	3
☹ Whole-wheat regular	2 - 5 ($^3/_4$ oz.)
☺ Whole-wheat lower fat or crispbreads	2 - 5 ($^3/_4$ oz.)
GRAHAM CRACKER, 2$^1/_2$-inch square	3
MATZOH	$^3/_4$ oz.
MELBA TOAST, about 2 x 4 inches	4 pieces
OYSTER CRACKERS	20
POPCORN	
☹ ☺ With butter	3 cups
☺ No fat added	3 cups
☺ Lower fat	3 cups
PRETZELS	$^3/_4$ oz.
RICE CAKES, 4 inches across	2
SNACK CHIPS	
Fat-free or baked (tortilla, potato), baked pita chips	15 - 20 ($^3/_4$ oz.)
☹ Regular (tortilla, potato)	9 - 13 ($^3/_4$ oz.)

BEANS, PEAS & LENTILS

The choices on this list count as 1 Starch + 1 Lean Meat

Food List	Serving Size
☺ BAKED BEANS	$^1/_3$ cup
☺ BEANS, cooked Black, Garbanzo, Kidney, Lima, Navy, Pinto, White	$^1/_2$ cup
☺ LENTILS, cooked Brown, Green, Yellow	$^1/_2$ cup
☺ PEAS, cooked Black-Eyed, Split	$^1/_2$ cup
✏ ☺ REFRIED BEANS, canned	$^1/_2$ cup

Note: BEANS, PEAS & LENTILS are also found on the PLANT-BASED PROTEINS list, page 187.

FRUITS

The weight listed includes skin, core, seeds, and rind.

Food List	Serving Size
APPLE, unpeeled, small Dried	1 (4 oz.) 4 rings
APPLESAUCE. unsweetened	1/2 cup
☺ APRICOTS Canned Dried	4 (5 1/2 oz.) 1/2 cup 8 halves
BANANA, extra small	1 (4 oz.)
☺ BLACKBERRIES	3/4 cup
BLUEBERRIES	3/4 cup
CANTALOUPE, small	1/3 melon or 1 cup cubed (11 oz.)
CHERRIES, sweet Sweet, canned	12 (3 oz.) 1/2 cup
DATES	3
DRIED FRUITS Blueberries, Cherries, Cranberries, Mixed Fruits, Raisins	2 tablespoons
☺ FIGS Dried	1 1/2 large or 2 medium (3 1/2 oz.) 1 1/2
FRUIT COCKTAIL	1/2 cup
GRAPEFRUIT, large Sections, canned	1/2 (11 oz.) 3/4 cup
GRAPES	17 (3 oz.)
HONEYDEW MELON	1 slice or 1 cup cubed (10 oz.)

Food List	Serving Size
☺ KIWI	1 (3$^{1}/_{2}$ oz.)
MANDARIN ORANGES, canned	$^{3}/_{4}$ cup
MANGO, small	$^{1}/_{2}$ fruit (5$^{1}/_{2}$ oz.) or $^{1}/_{2}$ cup
NECTARINE, small	1 (5 oz.)
☺ ORANGE, small	1 (6$^{1}/_{2}$ oz.)
PAPAYA	$^{1}/_{2}$ fruit (8 oz.) or 1 cup cubed
PEACHES, medium Canned	1 (6 oz.) $^{1}/_{2}$ cup
PEARS, large Canned	$^{1}/_{2}$ (4 oz.) $^{1}/_{2}$ cup
PINEAPPLE Canned	$^{3}/_{4}$ cup $^{1}/_{2}$ cup
PLUMS, small Canned Dried (Prunes)	2 (5 oz.) $^{1}/_{2}$ cup 3
☺ RASPBERRIES	1 cup
☺ STRAWBERRIES	1$^{1}/_{4}$ cups
☺ TANGERINES, small	2 (8 oz.)
WATERMELON	1 slice (13$^{1}/_{2}$ oz.) or 1$^{1}/_{4}$ cups cubed

Food List	Serving Size
APPLE JUICE / CIDER	$^{1}/_{2}$ cup
FRUIT JUICE BLENDS, 100% juice	$^{1}/_{3}$ cup
GRAPE JUICE	$^{1}/_{3}$ cup
GRAPEFRUIT JUICE	$^{1}/_{2}$ cup
ORANGE JUICE	$^{1}/_{2}$ cup
PINEAPPLE JUICE	$^{1}/_{2}$ cup
PRUNE JUICE	$^{1}/_{3}$ cup

MILK & YOGURTS

Food List	Serving Size	Count as
FAT-FREE OR LOW-FAT (1%)		
MILK, BUTTERMILK, ACIDOPHILUS MILK, LACTAID	1 cup	1 fat-free milk
EVAPORATED MILK	$^1/_2$ cup	1 fat-free milk
YOGURT, Plain or flavored, with an artificial sweetener	$^2/_3$ cup (6 oz.)	1 fat-free milk
REDUCED-FAT (2%)		
MILK, KEFIR, ACIDOPHILUS MILK, LACTAID	1 cup	1 reduced-fat milk
YOGURT, plain (6 oz.)	$^2/_3$ cup	1 reduced-fat milk
WHOLE		
MILK, BUTTERMILK, GOAT'S MILK	1 cup	1 whole milk
EVAPORATED MILK	$^1/_2$ cup	1 whole milk
YOGURT, plain	8 oz.	1 whole milk

Note: Two types of milk products are found on other lists: CHEESES are on the MEAT & MEAT SUBSTITUTES list (because they are rich in protein); CREAM and other dairy fats are on the FATS list.

DAIRY-LIKE FOODS

Food List	Serving Size	Count as
CHOCOLATE MILK		
Fat-free	1 cup	1 fat-free milk + 1 carbohydrate
Whole	1 cup	1 whole milk + 1 carbohydrate
EGGNOG, whole milk	$^1/_2$ cup	1 carbohydrate + 2 fats
RICE DRINK		
Flavored, low-fat	1 cup	2 carbohydrates
Plain, fat-free	1 cup	1 carbohydrate
SMOOTHIES		
Flavored, regular	10 oz.	1 fat-free milk + 2$^1/_2$ carbohydrates
SOY MILK		
Light	1 cup	1 carbohydrate + $^1/_2$ fat
Regular, plain	1 cup	1 carbohydrate + 1 fat
YOGURT & JUICE BLENDS	1 cup	1 fat-free milk + 1 carbohydrate
Low carbohydrate (less than 6 grams)	$^2/_3$ cup (6 oz.)	$^1/_2$ fat-free milk
With fruit, low-fat	$^2/_3$ cup (6 oz.)	1 fat-free milk + 1 carbohydrate

NONSTARCHY VEGETABLES

AMARANTH or CHINESE SPINACH

ARTICHOKE

ARTICHOKE HEARTS

ASPARAGUS

BABY CORN

BAMBOO SHOOTS

BEANS Green, Wax, Italian

BEAN SPROUTS

BEETS

🖉 BORSCHT

BROCCOLI

☺ BRUSSELS SPROUTS

CABBAGE Green, Bok Choy, Chinese

CARROTS

CELERY

☺ CHAYOTE

COLESLAW, packaged, no dressing

CUCUMBER

EGGPLANT

GOURDS Bitter, Bottle, Luffa, Bitter Melon

GREEN ONIONS or SCALLIONS

GREENS Collard, Kale, Mustard, Turnip

HEARTS OF PALM

JICAMA

KOHLRABI

LEEKS

MIXED VEGETABLES, without Corn, Peas or Pasta

MUNG BEAN SPROUTS

MUSHROOMS, all kind, fresh

OKRA

ONIONS

ORIENTAL RADISH or DAIKON

PEA PODS

PEPPERS, all varieties

RADISHES

RUTABAGA

🖉 SAUERKRAUT

SOYBEAN SPROUTS

SPINACH

SQUASH Summer, Crookneck, Zucchini

SUGAR SNAP PEAS

☺ SWISS CHARD

TOMATO

TOMATOES, canned

🖉 TOMATO, sauce, vegetable juice

TURNIPS

WATER CHESTNUTS

YARD-LONG BEANS

SPREADS, SWEETS, SWEETENERS, SYRUPS & TOPPINGS

Food List	Serving Size	Count as
FRUIT SPREADS, 100% fruit	1 1/2 tablespoons	1 carbohydrate
HONEY	1 tablespoon	1 carbohydrate
JAM OR JELLY, Regular	1 tablespoon	1 carbohydrate
SUGAR	1 tablespoon	1 carbohydrate

MEAT & MEAT SUBSTITUTES

Meat and meat substitutes are rich in protein. Foods from this list are divided into 4 groups based on the amount of fat they contain. These groups are LEAN MEAT, MEDIUM-FAT MEAT, HIGH-FAT MEAT and PLANT-BASED PROTEINS.

LEAN MEATS & MEAT SUBSTITUTES

Food List	Amount
BEEF Select or Choice grades trimmed of fat: Ground Round, Roast (Chuck, Rib, Rump), Round, Sirloin, Steak (Cubed, Flank, Porterhouse, T-Bone), Tenderloin	1 oz.
⬧ BEEF JERKY	1 oz.
CHEESES with 3 grams of fat or less	1 oz.
COTTAGE CHEESE	¼ cup
EGG SUBSTITUTES, plain	¼ cup
EGG WHITES	2
⬧ FISH, fresh or frozen, plain Catfish, Cod, Flounder, Haddock, Halibut, Orange Roughy, Salmon, Tilapia, Trout, Tuna	1 oz.
FISH, smoked Herring, Salmon (Lox)	1 oz.
GAME Buffalo, Ostrich, Rabbit, Venison	1 oz.
⬧ HOT DOG with 3 grams of fat or less per oz. (8 dogs per 14-oz. package) *Note:* May be high in carbohydrate	1
LAMB Chop, Leg or Roast	1 oz.
ORGAN MEATS Heart, Kidney, Liver *Note:* May be high in cholesterol	1 oz.
OYSTERS, fresh or frozen	6 medium

Food List	Amount
⬧ PORK, lean Canadian Bacon Rib or Loin Chop, Roast, Ham, Tenderloin	1 oz. 1 oz.
POULTRY, without skin Cornish Hen, Chicken, Domestic Duck or Goose (well-drained of fat), Turkey	1 oz.
PROCESSED SANDWICH MEATS with 3 grams of fat or less per oz. Chipped Beef, Deli Thin-Sliced Meats, Turkey Ham, Turkey Kielbasa, Turkey Pastrami	1 oz.
SALMON, canned	1 oz.
SARDINES, canned	1 oz.
⬧ SAUSAGE with 3 grams of fat or less per oz.	1 oz.
SHELLFISH Clams, Crab, Imitation Shellfish, Lobster, Scallops, Shrimp	1 oz.
TUNA, canned in water or oil, drained	1 oz.
VEAL Lean Chop, Roast	1 oz.

MEDIUM-FAT MEATS & MEAT SUBSTITUTES

Food List	Amount
BEEF Corned Beef, Ground Beef, Meatloaf, Prime grades trimmed of fat (Prime Rib), Short Ribs, Tongue	1 oz.
CHEESES with 4-7 grams of fat per oz. Feta, Mozzarella, Pasteurized Processed Cheese Spread, Reduced-Fat Cheeses, String	1 oz.
EGG Note: High in cholesterol, so limit to 3 per week	1
FISH, any fried product	1 oz.
LAMB Ground, Rib Roast	1 oz.
PORK Cutlet, Shoulder Roast	1 oz.
POULTRY Chicken with skin, Dove, Pheasant, Wild Duck or Goose, Fried Chicken, Ground Turkey	1 oz.
RICOTTA CHEESE	2 oz. or 1/4 cup
SAUSAGE with 4-7 grams of fat per oz.	1 oz.
VEAL Cutlet (no breading)	1 oz.

HIGH-FAT MEATS & MEAT SUBSTITUTES

Food List	Amount
BACON Pork	2 slices (16 slices per lb. or 1 oz. each, before cooking)
Turkey	3 slices (1/2 oz. each, before cooking)
CHEESE, regular American, Bleu, Brie, Cheddar, Hard Goat, Monterey Jack, Queso, Swiss	1 oz.
HOT DOG 10 dogs per 1-lb. package Beef, Pork, or combination	1
HOT DOG 10 dogs per 1-lb. package Turkey or Chicken	1
PORK Ground, Sausage, Spareribs	1 oz.
PROCESSED SANDWICH MEATS with 8 grams of fat or more per oz Bologna, Pastrami, Hard Salami	1 oz.
SAUSAGE with 8 grams fat or more per oz. Bratwurst, Chorizo, Italian, Knockwurst, Polish, Smoked, Summer	1 oz.

These foods are high in saturated fat, cholesterol, and calories and may raise blood cholesterol levels if eaten on a regular basis. Try to eat 3 or fewer servings from this group per week.

PLANT-BASED PROTEINS

Because carbohydrate content varies among plant-based proteins, you should read the food label.

Food List	Serving Size	Count as
"BACON" STRIPS, soy-based	3 strips	1 medium-fat meat
☺ BAKED BEANS	½ cup	1 starch + 1 lean meat
☺ BEANS, cooked Black, Garbanzo, Kidney, Lima, Navy, Pinto, White	½ cup	1 starch + 1 lean meat
☺ "BEEF" or "SAUSAGE" CRUMBLES, soy-based	2 oz.	½ carbohydrate + 1 lean meat
"CHICKEN" NUGGETS, soy-based	2 nuggets (1½ oz.)	½ carbohydrate + 1 medium-fat meat
☺ EDAMAME	½ cup	½ carbohydrate +1 lean meat
FALAFEL (spiced chickpea & wheat patties)	3 patties (about 2 inches across)	1 carbohydrate + 1 high-fat meat
HOT DOG, soy-based	1 (1½ oz.)	½ carbohydrate + 1 lean meat
☺ HUMMUS	⅓ cup	1 carbohydrate + 1 high-fat meatt
☺ LENTILS, Brown, Green, Yellow	½ cup	1 carbohydrate + 1 lean meat
☺ MEATLESS BURGER, soy-based	3 oz.	½ carbohydrate + 2 lean meat
☺ MEATLESS BURGER, vegetable and starch-based	1 patty (about 2½ oz.)	1 carbohydrate + 2 lean meat
NUT SPREADS Almond Butter, Cashew Butter, Peanut Butter, Soy Nut Butter	1 tablespoon	1 high-fat meat
☺ PEAS, cooked Black-Eyed and Split Peas	½ cup	1 starch + 1 lean meat
🖉 ☺ REFRIED BEANS, canned	½ cup	1 starch + 1 lean meat
"SAUSAGE" PATTIES, soy-based	1 (1½ oz.)	1 medium-fat meat
SOY NUTS, unsalted	¾ oz.	½ carbohydrate + 1 medium-fat meat
TEMPEH	¼ cup	1 medium-fat meat
TOFU	4 oz. (½ cup)	1 medium-fat meat
TOFU, light	4 oz. (½ cup)	1 lean meat

FATS

Fats and oils have mixtures of UNSATURATED (POLYUNSATURATED and MONOUNSATURATED) and SATURATED FATS.

Foods on the Fats list are grouped together based on the major type of fat they contain. In general, 1 fat choice equals:

= 1 teaspoon of regular margarine, vegetable oil, or butter
= 1 tablespoon of regular salad dressing

UNSATURATED FATS – MONOUNSATURATED FATS

Food List	Serving Size
AVOCADO, medium	2 tablespoons (1 oz.)
NUT BUTTERS, trans fat free Almond Butter, Cashew Butter, Peanut Butter (smooth or crunchy)	1½ teaspoons
NUTS	
Almonds	6 nuts
Brazil	2 nuts
Cashews	6 nuts
Filberts (Hazelnuts)	5 nuts
Macadamia	3 nuts
Mixed (50% Peanuts)	6 nuts
Peanuts	10 nuts
Pecans	4 halves
Pistachios	16 nuts
OIL Canola, Olive, Peanut	1 teaspoon
OLIVES	
Black (Ripe)	8 large
Green (Stuffed)	10 large

UNSATURATED FATS – POLYUNSATURATED FATS

Food List	Serving Size
MARGARINE, lower fat spread (30%-50% vegetable oil, trans fat free)	1 tablespoon
MARGARINE Stick, Tub or Squeeze (trans fat free)	1 teaspoon
MAYONNAISE Reduced-fat	1 tablespoon
Regular	1 teaspoon
MAYONNAISE-STYLE SALAD DRESSING Reduced-fat	1 tablespoon
Regular	2 teaspoons
NUTS Pignolia (Pine Nuts)	1 tablespoon
Walnuts, English	4 halves
OIL Corn, Cottonseed, Flaxseed, Grape Seed, Safflower, Soybean, Sunflower	1 teaspoon
OIL Made from soybean and Canola Oil – Enova	1 teaspoon
PLANT STANOL ESTERS Light	1 tablespoon
Regular	2 teaspoons
SALAD DRESSING Reduced-fat	2 tablespoons
Note: May be high in carbohydrate Regular	1 tablespoon
SEEDS Flaxseed, whole	1 tablespoon
Pumpkin, Sunflower	1 tablespoon
Sesame Seeds	1 tablespoon
TAHINI OF SESAME PASTE	2 teaspoons

SATURATED FATS

Food List	Serving Size
BACON, cooked, regular or turkey	1 slice
BUTTER Reduced-fat	1 tablespoon
Stick	1 teaspoon
Whipped	2 teaspoons
BUTTER BLENDS MADE WITH OIL Reduced-fat or light	1 tablespoon
Regular	1 1/2 teaspoons
CHITTERLINGS, boiled	2 tablespoons (1/2 oz.)
COCONUT, sweetened, shredded	2 tablespoons
COCONUT MILK Light	1/3 cup
Regular	1 1/2 tablespoons
CREAM Half and half	2 tablespoons
Heavy	1 tablespoon
Light	1 1/2 tablespoons
Whipped	2 tablespoons
Whipped, pressurized	1/4 cup
CREAM CHEESE Reduced-fat	1 1/2 tblspns (3/4 oz.)
Regular	1 tablespoon (1/2 oz.)
LARD	1 teaspoon
OIL Coconut, Palm, Palm Kernel	1 teaspoon
SALT PORK	1/4 oz.
SHORTENING, solid	1 teaspoon
SOUR CREAM Reduced-fat or light	3 tablespoons
Regular	2 tablespoons

CONVERSION CHARTS

Standard United States measures are used for the recipes in this cookbook. The information presented in the following Conversion Charts can be used to determine *approximate* metric equivalents.

METRIC EQUIVALENTS
FOR DIFFERENT TYPES OF INGREDIENTS

A standard cup measure of a dry or solid ingredient will vary in weight depending on the type of ingredient.
A standard cup of liquid is the same volume for any type of liquid.
Use the following chart when converting standard cup measures to grams (weight) or milliliters (volume).

Standard Cup	Fine Powder (ex. flour)	Grain (ex.rice)	Granular (ex. sugar)	Liquid Solids (ex. butter)	Liquid (ex. milk)
1	= 140 g	= 150 g	= 190 g	= 200 g	= 240 ml
3/4	= 105 g	= 113 g	= 143 g	= 150 g	= 180 ml
2/3	= 93 g	= 100 g	= 125 g	= 133 g	= 160 ml
1/2	= 70 g	= 75 g	= 95 g	= 100 g	= 120 ml
1/3	= 47 g	= 50 g	= 63 g	= 67 g	= 80 ml
1/4	= 35 g	= 38 g	= 48 g	= 50 g	= 60 ml
1/8	= 18 g	= 19 g	= 24 g	= 25 g	= 30 ml

USEFUL EQUIVALENTS
FOR DRY INGREDIENTS BY WEIGHT

To convert ounces to grams,
multiply the number of ounces by 30

1 oz	= 1/16 lb	= 30 g
4 oz	= 1/4 lb	= 120 g
8 oz	= 1/2 lb	= 240 g
12 oz	= 3/4 lb	= 360 g
16 oz	= 1 lb	= 480 g

USEFUL EQUIVALENTS
FOR LENGTH

To convert inches to centimeters,
multiply number of inches by 2 1/2

1 in		= 2 1/2 cm	
6 in	= 1/2 ft	= 15 cm	
12 in	= 1 ft	= 30 cm	
36 in	= 3 ft	= 1 yd	= 90 cm
40 in		= 100 cm	= 1 m

USEFUL EQUIVALENTS
FOR COOKING/OVEN TEMPERATURES

	Fahrenheit	Celsius	Gas Mark
Freeze Water	32° F	= 0° C	
Room Temperature	68° F	= 20° C	
Boil Water	212° F	= 100° C	
Bake	325° F	= 160° C	= 3
	350° F	= 180° C	= 4
	375° F	= 190° C	= 5
	400° F	= 200° C	= 6
	425° F	= 220° C	= 7
	450° F	= 230° C	= 8
Broil			= Grill

USEFUL EQUIVALENTS
FOR LIQUID INGREDIENTS BY VOLUME

1/4 tsp				= 1 ml
1/2 tsp				= 2 ml
1 tsp				= 5 ml
3 tsp	= 1 tbls		= 1/2 fl oz	= 15 ml
	2 tbls	= 1/8 cup	= 1 fl oz	= 30 ml
	4 tbls	= 1/4 cup	= 2 fl oz	= 60 ml
	5 1/3 tbls	= 1/3 cup	= 3 fl oz	= 80 ml
	8 tbls	= 1/2 cup	= 4 fl oz	= 120 ml
	10 2/3 tbls	= 2/3 cup	= 5 fl oz	= 160 ml
	12 tbls	= 3/4 cup	= 6 fl oz	= 180 ml
	16 tbls	= 1 cup	= 8 fl oz	= 240 ml
	1 pt	= 2 cups	= 16 fl oz	= 480 ml
	1 qt	= 4 cups	= 32 fl oz	= 960 ml
			33 fl oz	= 1000 ml
				(1 liter)

INDEX